Microsoft® Excel 2000
Introductory Edition

INTERACTIVE COMPUTING SERIES

Kenneth C. Laudon
Kenneth Rosenblatt

with Michael W. Domis

Azimuth Interactive, Inc.

Boston   Burr Ridge, IL   Dubuque, IA   Madison, WI   New York   San Francisco   St. Louis
Bangkok   Bogotá   Caracas   Lisbon   London   Madrid   Mexico City   Milan   New Delhi   Seoul
Singapore   Sydney   Taipei   Toronto

McGraw-Hill Higher Education

*A Division of The **McGraw-Hill** Companies*

MICROSOFT EXCEL 2000 INTRODUCTORY EDITION
Copyright © 2000 by The McGraw-Hill Companies, Inc. All rights reserved. Printed in the United States of America. Except as permitted under the United States Copyright Act of 1976, no part of this publication may be reproduced or distributed in any form or by any means, or stored in a data base or retrieval system, without the prior written permission of the publisher.

 This book is printed on recycled, acid-free paper containing 10% postconsumer waste.

2 3 4 5 6 7 8 9 0 QPD/QPD 9 0 9 8 7 6 5 4 3 2 1 0 9

ISBN 0-07-234930-1

Vice president/Editor-in-Chief: *Michael W. Junior*
Sponsoring editor: *Trisha O'Shea*
Developmental editor: *Kyle Thomes*
Senior marketing manager: *Jodi McPherson*
Project manager: *Carrie Sestak*
Production supervisor: *Michael R. McCormick*
Senior freelance design coordinator: *Laurie Entringer*
Supplement coordinator: *Matthew Perry*
Compositor: *Azimuth Interactive, Inc.*
Typeface: *10/12 Sabon*
Printer: *Quebecor Printing Book Group/Dubuque*

Library of Congress Catalog Card Number: 99-64193

http://www.mhhe.com

Microsoft® Excel 2000
Introductory Edition

INTERACTIVE COMPUTING SERIES

Kenneth C. Laudon
Kenneth Rosenblatt

with Michael W. Domis

Azimuth Interactive, Inc.

At **McGraw-Hill Higher Education**, we publish instructional materials targeted at the higher education market. In an effort to expand the tools of higher learning, we publish texts, lab manuals, study guides, testing materials, software, and multimedia products.

At **Irwin/McGraw-Hill** (a division of McGraw-Hill Higher Education), we realize technology will continue to create new mediums for professors and students to manage resources and communicate information with one another. We strive to provide the most flexible and complete teaching and learning tools available and offer solutions to the changing world of teaching and learning.

Irwin/McGraw-Hill is dedicated to providing the tools necessary for today's instructors and students to navigate the world of Information Technology successfully.

Seminar Series - Irwin/McGraw-Hill's Technology Connection seminar series offered across the country every year, demonstrates the latest technology products and encourages collaboration among teaching professionals.

Osborne/McGraw-Hill - A division of the McGraw-Hill Companies known for its best-selling Internet titles *Harley Hahn's Internet & Web Yellow Pages* and the *Internet Complete Reference*, offers an additional resource for certification and has strategic publishing relationships with corporations such as Corel Corporation and America Online. For more information, visit Osborne at www.osborne.com.

Digital Solutions - Irwin/McGraw-Hill is committed to publishing Digital Solutions. Taking your course online doesn't have to be a solitary venture. Nor does it have to be a difficult one. We offer several solutions, which will let you enjoy all the benefits of having course material online. For more information, visit www.mhhe.com/solutions/index.mhtml.

Packaging Options - For more about our discount options, contact your local Irwin/McGraw-Hill Sales representative at 1-800-338-3987, or visit our Web site at www.mhhe.com/it.

Preface

Interactive Computing Series

Goals/Philosophy

The *Interactive Computing Series* provides you with an illustrated interactive environment for learning software skills using Microsoft Office. The Interactive Computing Series is composed of both text and multimedia interactive CD-ROMs. The text and the CD-ROMs are closely coordinated. *It's up to you. You can choose how you want to learn.*

Approach

The *Interactive Computing Series* is the visual interactive way to develop and apply software skills. This skills-based approach coupled with its highly visual, two-page spread design allows the student to focus on a single skill without having to turn the page. A running case study is provided through the text, reinforcing the skills and giving a real-world focus to the learning process.

About the Book

APPROVED COURSEWARE
Level 1
Microsoft® Office User Specialist
Excel 2000 Exam

The **Interactive Computing Series** offers *two levels* of instruction. Each level builds upon the previous level.

Brief lab manual - covers the basics of the application, contains two to four chapters.
Introductory lab manual - includes the material in the Brief textbook plus two to four additional chapters. The Introductory lab manuals prepare students for the *Microsoft Office User Specialist Proficiency Exam (MOUS Certification)*.

Each lesson is organized around **Skills**, **Concepts**, and **Steps (Do It!)**.

Each lesson is divided into a number of Skills. Each **Skill** is first explained at the top of the page.
Each **Concept** is a concise description of why the skill is useful and where it is commonly used.
Each **Step (Do It!)** contains the instructions on how to complete the skill.

About the CD-ROM

The CD-ROM provides a unique interactive environment for students where they learn to use software faster and remember it better. The CD-ROM is organized in a similar approach as the text: The **Skill** is defined, the **Concept** is explained in rich multimedia, and the student performs **Steps (Do It!)** within sections called Interactivities. There are at least <u>45 Interactivities per CD-ROM</u>. Some of the features of the CD-ROM are:

Simulated Environment - The Interactive Computing CD-ROM places students in a simulated controlled environment where they can practice and perform the skills of the application software.
Interactive Exercises - The student is asked to demonstrate command of a specific software skill. The student's actions are followed by a digital "TeacherWizard" that provides feedback.
SmartQuizzes - Provide performance-based assessment of the student at the end of each lesson.

Using the Book

In the book, each skill is described in a two-page graphical spread (Figure 1). The left side of the two-page spread describes the skill, the concept, and the steps needed to perform the skill. The right side of the spread uses screen shots to show you how the screen should look at key stages.

Figure 1

Skill: Each lesson is divided into a number of specific skills

Concept: A concise description of why the skill is useful and where it is commonly used

Running case: A real-world case ties the skill and the concept to a practical situation

Do It!: Step-by-step directions show you how to use the skill

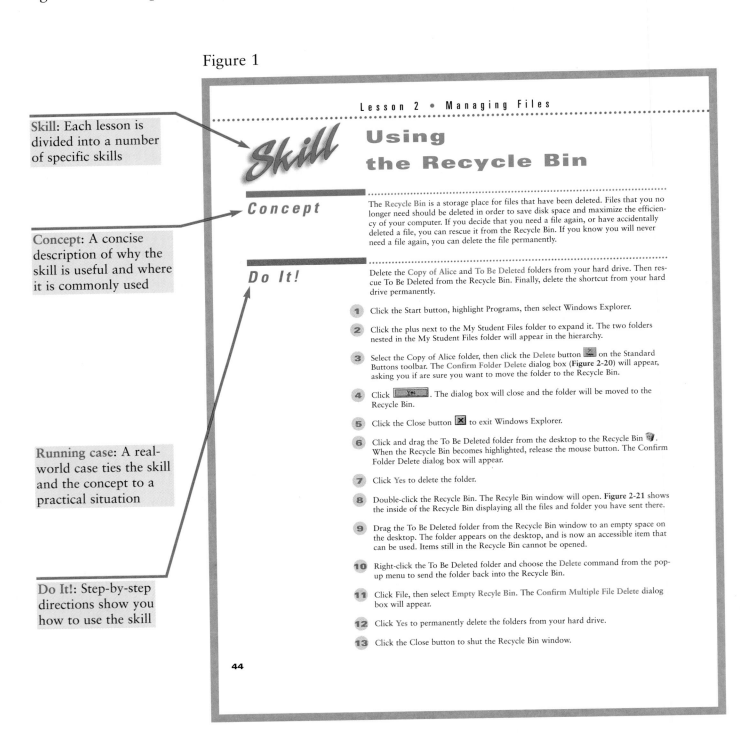

Lesson 2 • Managing Files

Skill
Using the Recycle Bin

Concept

The Recycle Bin is a storage place for files that have been deleted. Files that you no longer need should be deleted in order to save disk space and maximize the efficiency of your computer. If you decide that you need a file again, or have accidentally deleted a file, you can rescue it from the Recycle Bin. If you know you will never need a file again, you can delete the file permanently.

Do It!

Delete the Copy of Alice and To Be Deleted folders from your hard drive. Then rescue To Be Deleted from the Recycle Bin. Finally, delete the shortcut from your hard drive permanently.

1. Click the Start button, highlight Programs, then select Windows Explorer.

2. Click the plus next to the My Student Files folder to expand it. The two folders nested in the My Student Files folder will appear in the hierarchy.

3. Select the Copy of Alice folder, then click the Delete button 🗙 on the Standard Buttons toolbar. The Confirm Folder Delete dialog box (**Figure 2-20**) will appear, asking you if are sure you want to move the folder to the Recycle Bin.

4. Click ⬚Yes⬚. The dialog box will close and the folder will be moved to the Recycle Bin.

5. Click the Close button 🗙 to exit Windows Explorer.

6. Click and drag the To Be Deleted folder from the desktop to the Recycle Bin 🗑. When the Recycle Bin becomes highlighted, release the mouse button. The Confirm Folder Delete dialog box will appear.

7. Click Yes to delete the folder.

8. Double-click the Recycle Bin. The Recyle Bin window will open. **Figure 2-21** shows the inside of the Recycle Bin displaying all the files and folder you have sent there.

9. Drag the To Be Deleted folder from the Recycle Bin window to an empty space on the desktop. The folder appears on the desktop, and is now an accessible item that can be used. Items still in the Recycle Bin cannot be opened.

10. Right-click the To Be Deleted folder and choose the Delete command from the pop-up menu to send the folder back into the Recycle Bin.

11. Click File, then select Empty Recycle Bin. The Confirm Multiple File Delete dialog box will appear.

12. Click Yes to permanently delete the folders from your hard drive.

13. Click the Close button to shut the Recycle Bin window.

44

End-of-Lesson Features

In the book, the learning in each lesson is reinforced at the end by a quiz and a skills review called Interactivity, which provides step-by-step exercises and real-world problems for the students to solve independently.

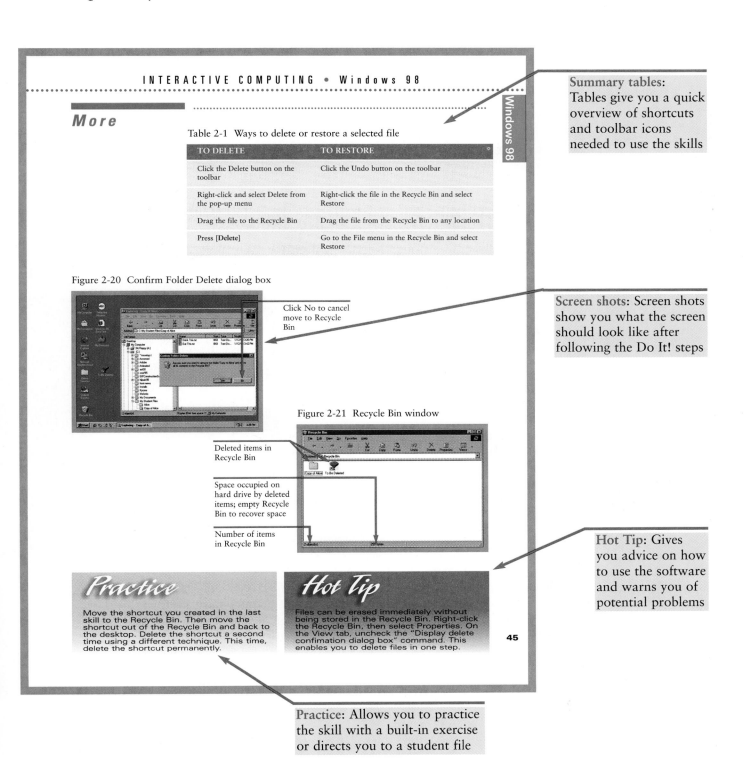

INTERACTIVE COMPUTING • Windows 98

Windows 98

More

Table 2-1 Ways to delete or restore a selected file

TO DELETE	TO RESTORE
Click the Delete button on the toolbar	Click the Undo button on the toolbar
Right-click and select Delete from the pop-up menu	Right-click the file in the Recycle Bin and select Restore
Drag the file to the Recycle Bin	Drag the file from the Recycle Bin to any location
Press [Delete]	Go to the File menu in the Recycle Bin and select Restore

Figure 2-20 Confirm Folder Delete dialog box

Click No to cancel move to Recycle Bin

Figure 2-21 Recycle Bin window

Deleted items in Recycle Bin

Space occupied on hard drive by deleted items; empty Recycle Bin to recover space

Number of items in Recycle Bin

Practice

Move the shortcut you created in the last skill to the Recycle Bin. Then move the shortcut out of the Recycle Bin and back to the desktop. Delete the shortcut a second time using a different technique. This time, delete the shortcut permanently.

Hot Tip

Files can be erased immediately without being stored in the Recycle Bin. Right-click the Recycle Bin, then select Properties. On the View tab, uncheck the "Display delete confimation dialog box" command. This enables you to delete files in one step.

45

Summary tables: Tables give you a quick overview of shortcuts and toolbar icons needed to use the skills

Screen shots: Screen shots show you what the screen should look like after following the Do It! steps

Hot Tip: Gives you advice on how to use the software and warns you of potential problems

Practice: Allows you to practice the skill with a built-in exercise or directs you to a student file

Using the Interactive CD-ROM

The Interactive Computing multimedia CD-ROM provides an unparalleled learning environment in which you can learn software skills faster and better than in books alone. The CD-ROM creates a unique interactive environment in which you can learn to use software faster and remember it better. The CD-ROM uses the same lessons, skills, concepts, and Do It! steps as found in the book, but presents the material using voice, video, animation, and precise simulation of the software you are learning. A typical CD-ROM contents screen shows the major elements of a lesson (see Figure 2 below).

Skills list: A list of skills allows you to jump directly to any skill you want to learn or review, including interactive sessions with the TeacherWizard

Figure 2

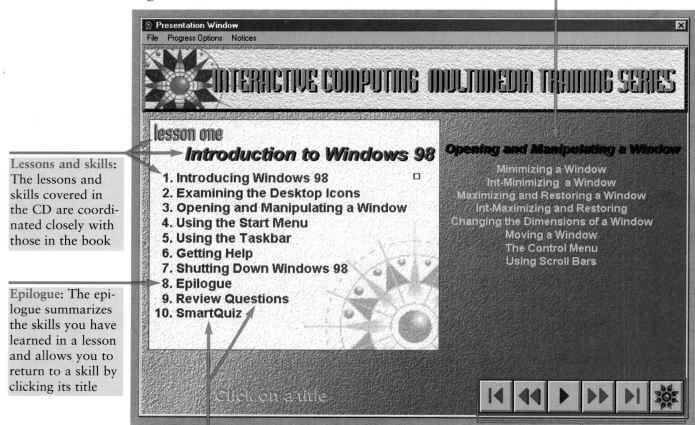

Lessons and skills: The lessons and skills covered in the CD are coordinated closely with those in the book

Epilogue: The epilogue summarizes the skills you have learned in a lesson and allows you to return to a skill by clicking its title

Review Questions and **SmartQuiz:** Review Questions test your knowledge of the concepts covered in the lesson; SmartQuiz tests your ability to accomplish tasks in a simulated software environment

User controls: Precise and simple user controls permit you to start, stop, pause, jump forward or backward one sentence, or jump forward or backward an entire skill. A single navigation star takes you back to the lesson's table of contents

Unique Features of the CD-ROM: TeacherWizard™ and SmartQuiz™

Interactive Computing: Software Skills offers many leading-edge features on the CD currently found in no other learning product on the market. One such feature is *interactive exercises* in which you are asked to demonstrate your command of a software skill in a precisely simulated software environment. Your actions are followed closely by a digital TeacherWizard that guides you with additional information if you make a mistake. When you complete the action called for by the TeacherWizard correctly, you are congratulated and prompted to continue the lesson. If you make a mistake, the TeacherWizard gently lets you know: "No, that's not the right icon. Click on the Folder icon on the left side of the top toolbar to open a file." No matter how many mistakes you make, the TeacherWizard is there to help you.

Another leading-edge feature is the end-of-lesson SmartQuiz. Unlike the multiple choice and matching questions found in the book quiz, the SmartQuiz puts you in a simulated digital software world and asks you to show your mastery of skills while actually working with the software (Figure 3).

Figure 3

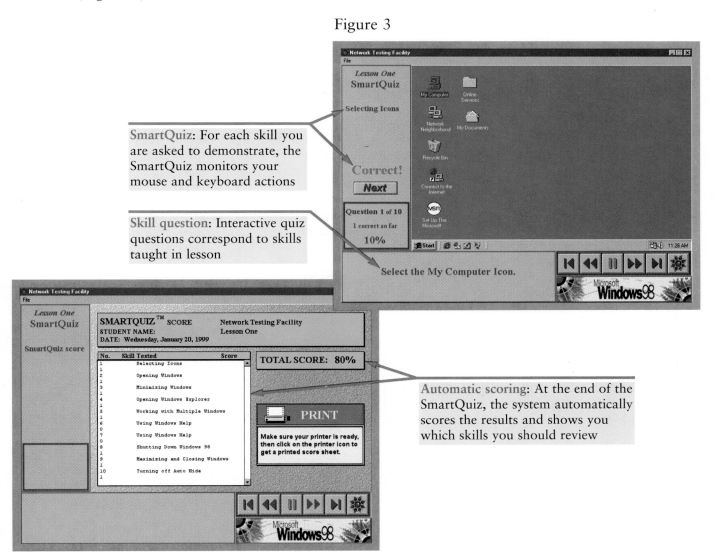

SmartQuiz: For each skill you are asked to demonstrate, the SmartQuiz monitors your mouse and keyboard actions

Skill question: Interactive quiz questions correspond to skills taught in lesson

Automatic scoring: At the end of the SmartQuiz, the system automatically scores the results and shows you which skills you should review

Teaching Resources

The following is a list of supplemental material available with the *Interactive Computing Series*:

Skills Assessment

Irwin/McGraw-Hill offers two innovative systems, ATLAS and SimNet, which take testing beyond the basics with pre- and post-assessment capabilities.

ATLAS (Active Testing and Learning Assessment Software) – available for the *Interactive Computing Series* – is our live-in-the-application Skills Assessment tool. ATLAS allows students to perform tasks while working live within the Office applications environment. ATLAS is web-enabled and customizable to meet the needs of your course. ATLAS is available for Office 2000.

SimNet (Simulated Network Assessment Product) – available for the *Interactive Computing Series* – permits you to test the actual software skills students learn about the Microsoft Office applications in a simulated environment. SimNet is web-enabled and is available for Office 97 and Office 2000.

Instructor's Resource Kits

The Instructor's Resource Kit provides professors with all of the ancillary material needed to teach a course. Irwin/McGraw-Hill is dedicated to providing instructors with the most effective instruction resources available. Many of these resources are available at our **Information Technology Supersite** www.mhhe.com/it. Our Instructor's Kits are available on CD-ROM and contain the following:

> **Network Testing Facility (NTF)** - Tests acquired software skills in a safe simulated software environment. NTF tracks a student score and allows the instructor to build screens that indicate student progress.
>
> **Diploma by Brownstone** - is the most flexible, powerful, and easy-to-use computerized testing system available in higher education. The diploma system allows professors to create an Exam as a printed version, as a LAN-based Online version, and as an Internet version. Diploma includes grade book features, which automate the entire testing process.
>
> **Instructor's Manual** - Includes:
> -Solutions to all lessons and end-of-unit material
> -Teaching Tips
> -Teaching Strategies
> -Additional exercises
>
> **Student Data Files** - To use the Interactive Computing Series, students must have Student Data Files to complete practice and test sessions. The instructor and students using this text in classes are granted the right to post the student files on any network or stand-alone computer, or to distribute the files on individual diskettes. The student files may be downloaded from our IT Supersite at www.mhhe.com/it.
>
> **Series Web Site** - Available at www.mhhe.com/cit/apps/laudon.

Digital Solutions

> **Pageout Lite** - is designed if you're just beginning to explore Web site options. Pageout Lite is great for posting your own material online. You may choose one of three templates, type in your material, and Pageout Lite instantly converts it to HTML.
>
> **Pageout** - is our Course Web site Development Center. Pageout offers a Syllabus page, Web site address, Online Learning Center Content, online exercises and quizzes, gradebook, discussion board, an area for students to build their own Web pages, and all the features of Pageout Lite. For more information please visit the Pageout Web site at www.mhla.net/pageout.

Teaching Resources (continued)

OLC/Series Web Sites - Online Learning Centers (OLCs)/Series Sites are accessible through our Supersite at www.mhhe.com/it. Our Online Learning Centers/Series Sites provide pedagogical features and supplements for our titles online. Students can point and click their way to key terms, learning objectives, chapter overviews, PowerPoint slides, exercises, and web links.

The McGraw-Hill Learning Architecture (MHLA) - is a complete course delivery system. MHLA gives professors ownership in the way digital content is presented to the class through online quizzing, student collaboration, course administration, and content management. For a walk-through of MHLA visit the MHLA Web site at www.mhla.net.

Packaging Options - For more about our discount options, contact your local Irwin/McGraw-Hill Sales representative at 1-800-338-3987 or visit our Web site at www.mhhe.com/it.

Visit www.mhhe.com/it
THE ONLY SITE WITH ALL YOUR CIT AND MIS NEEDS.

Acknowledgments

The Interactive Computing Series is a cooperative effort of many individuals, each contributing to an overall team effort. The Interactive Computing team is composed of instructional designers, writers, multimedia designers, graphic artists, and programmers. Our goal is to provide you and your instructor with the most powerful and enjoyable learning environment using both traditional text and new interactive multimedia techniques. Interactive Computing is tested rigorously in both CD and text formats prior to publication.

Our special thanks to Trisha O'Shea and Kyle Lewis, our Editors for computer applications and concepts. Both Trisha and Kyle have poured their enthusiasm into the project and inspired us all to work closely together. Kyle Thomes, our Developmental Editor, has provided superb feedback from the market and excellent advice on content. Jodi McPherson, marketing, has added her inimitable enthusiasm and market knowledge. Finally, Mike Junior, Vice-President and Editor-in-Chief, provided the unstinting support required for a project of this magnitude.

The Azimuth team members who contributed to the textbooks and CD-ROM multimedia program are:

Ken Rosenblatt (Textbooks Project Manager and Writer, Interactive Writer)
Steven D. Pileggi (Interactive Project Manager, Writer)
Russell Polo (Programmer)
Raymond Wang (Multimedia Designer)
Michele Faranda (Textbook design and layout)
Jason Eiseman (Technical Writer, layout)
Michael Domis (Technical Writer)
Thomas Grande (Multimedia Designer)
Stefon Westry (Multimedia Designer)
Caroline Kasterine (Multimedia Designer, Writer)
Tahir Kahn (Multimedia Designer)
Joseph S. Gina (Multimedia Designer)
Irene A. Caruso (Multimedia Designer, Writer)

Contents

Excel 2000 Introductory Edition

Contents

Continued

Contents

Continued

L E S S O N

1

INTRODUCTION TO SPREADSHEET SOFTWARE

Microsoft Excel is a computer application that improves your ability to record data and then extract results from it. With Excel, you can enter text labels and numerical values into an electronic spreadsheet, a grid made up of columns and rows. The computerized worksheets you work with in Excel resemble handwritten ledgers with which you may already be familiar. Being able to use spreadsheet software can help you both professionally and personally. By providing an organized structure in which to work, Excel can increase the efficiency with which you conduct business and track your own affairs. Excel's ability to perform and automate calculations saves time and decreases the possibility of error.

Using Excel, you will learn how to create a spreadsheet employing proper design techniques. You will then explore the application and become familiar with its basic elements and operations. Later on, some of Excel's more advanced features such as formulas, What-if analysis, and macros will broaden your knowledge of how to create and work with a spreadsheet. If you need assistance while using Excel, the program includes an extensive help facility, as well as the ability to access online support via the World Wide Web.

CASE STUDY
Kay Samoy is the owner of a small but successful company that distributes a wide variety of dog accessories such as treats, furnishings, and toys. She would like to use Excel to track her income, expenses, and profits electronically now that her business is growing. Kay will begin by familiarizing herself with the application. Then she will take the first steps toward creating an effective spreadsheet.

Introducing Excel and Worksheet Design

Concept

Microsoft Excel is an electronic spreadsheet application designed to make the creation and use of professional quality spreadsheets fast and easy. A spreadsheet is a table composed of rows and columns that store text and numbers for easy viewing and tabulation. Electronic spreadsheets are very useful for performing rapid and accurate calculations on groups of interrelated numbers. Using Excel, you can:

- Organize information rapidly and accurately. With the proper data and formulas, Excel calculates your results automatically.

- Recalculate automatically. Fixing errors in Excel is easy. When you find a mistake and correct the entry, Excel automatically recalculates all related data.

- Keep track of the effect that changing one piece of data has on related numbers. You can postulate changes that may occur in the future and see how they could change the results of your calculations – a feature called What-If analysis.

- Display data as graphs or charts. Excel allows you to display numeric data graphically in the form of charts that are automatically updated as the data changes. For example, **Figure 1-1** shows the data in a spreadsheet for income and expenditures that can also be displayed in the form of a pie chart. Charts often make relationships among data easier to understand.

The spreadsheet's organization is shaped by its goal or purpose. A well-designed spreadsheet should be accurate, easily understood, and should include the four sections visible in **Figure 1-2**: documentation, assumptions, input, and results.

- The first section contains documentation, consisting of a complete description of the name of the author, the purpose of the spreadsheet, the date it was created, and the name of the spreadsheet file. Documentation should also specify location of any cell ranges and macros. Ranges are blocks of columns and rows that are useful for performing certain types of calculations and for displaying data. Macros are instructions for automating spreadsheet tasks.

- The second section of a spreadsheet is used to display assumptions. Assumptions are variable factors that may change in a worksheet. For example, Kay's profit projections assume that sales will expand by 10% each quarter. When her sales numbers are changed, they will affect the amount of profit. It is easier to change documented assumptions than undocumented ones. Assumptions are useful when conducting "what-if" analysis based on calculating the effect of changes in spreadsheet data. For instance, what if sales only grow by 5%? You will learn more about What-If analysis in Lesson 2.

- The third section of the spreadsheet stores input, the numbers that you enter and manipulate. In **Figure 1-2**, the input section contains data for income and expenditures. Input data is generally arranged in blocks of numbers organized in columns and rows.

- The fourth section is a results, or output section, which displays the results of the calculations made on the input data. Output data is generally placed below and to the right of input data.

More

Microsoft Excel stores each workbook you create as an individual document in the computer's memory. A document, also called a file, can be a single worksheet or may contain many of pages of data and graphs. Each file should be given a unique name so it can be easily differentiated from other files. Excel documents are given the file extension .xls. A file extension is a three letter code, separated from the file name with a period, called a dot, that tells the computer what application is associated with a particular file.

Figure 1-1 A worksheet made with Microsoft Excel

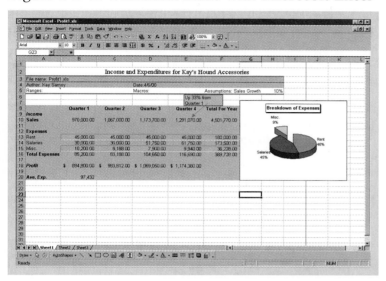

Excel 2000

Figure 1-2 Organization of a spreadsheet

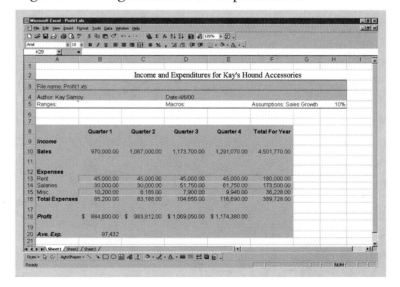

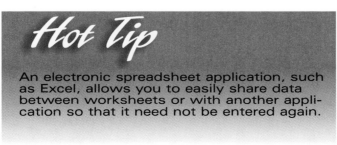

Hot Tip

An electronic spreadsheet application, such as Excel, allows you to easily share data between worksheets or with another application so that it need not be entered again.

Starting Excel

Concept

To use the Microsoft Excel program, or application, the user must first open it. The act of opening an application can also be called running, starting, or launching. In the Windows environment, you can launch a program in a number of ways, including using desktop and Start menu shortcuts, using the Run command, double-clicking executable file icons, and clicking a Windows 98 Quick Launch toolbar button.

Do It!

Kay wants to open the Microsoft Excel application so she can begin to construct a worksheet.

1. Make sure the computer, monitor and any other necessary peripheral devices are turned on. The Windows desktop should appear on your screen. Your screen may differ slightly from the one shown.

2. Locate the Windows taskbar, usually found at the bottom of your screen. Use the mouse to guide the pointer over the Start button, on the left side of the taskbar, and click [Start]. This will open the Windows Start menu.

3. Move the mouse pointer ⬚ up the Start menu to Programs, highlighting it. The Programs menu will be displayed as shown in **Figure 1-3**.

4. Position the pointer over Microsoft Excel to highlight it, and then click once to open the application. (If Excel is not there, try looking under Microsoft Office on the Start menu.) Excel will open with a blank worksheet in the window as shown in **Figure 1-4**.

More

Each computer can vary in its setup depending on its hardware and software configurations. Therefore, your Excel startup procedure may be slightly different from that described above. The Windows environment allows you to place shortcuts to a program's executable (.exe) file in various places. For example, the Excel listing on the Programs menu is a shortcut. You can also place shortcuts on the desktop, or even on the first level of the Start menu. Because you can customize the Excel program your screen may not look exactly like the one shown to the right.

Figure 1-3 Windows desktop and Start menu

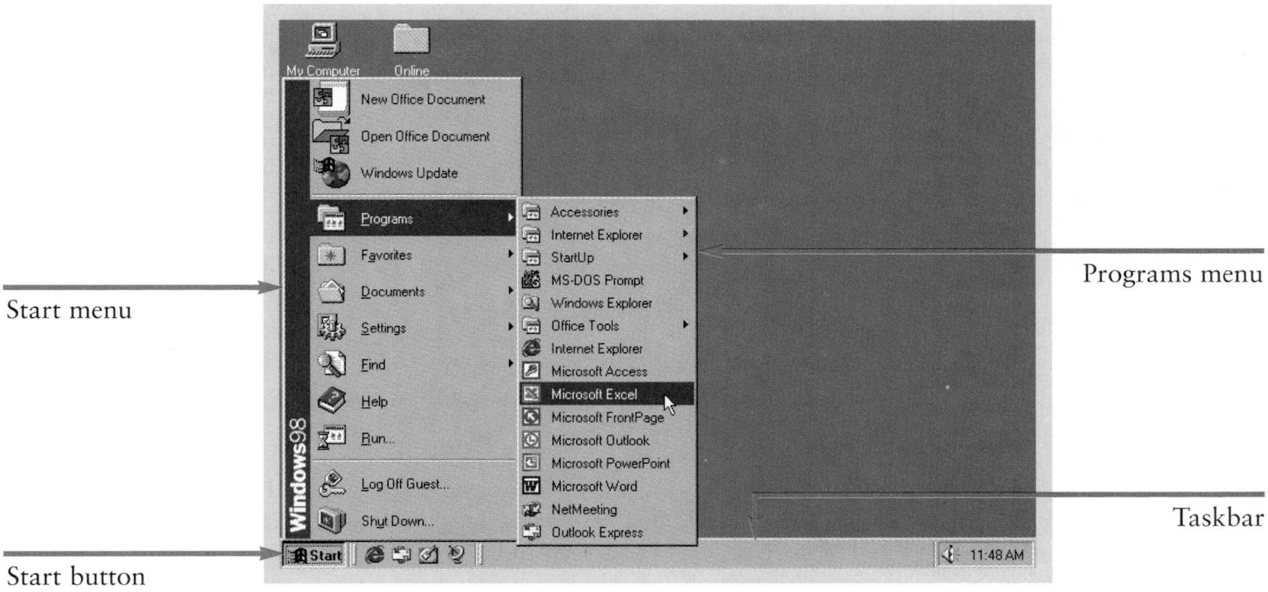

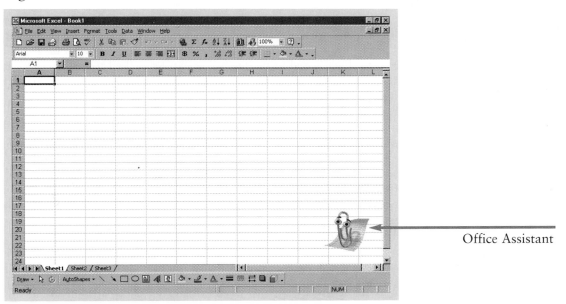

Start menu

Start button

Programs menu

Taskbar

Excel 2000

Figure 1-4 Excel window

Office Assistant

Hot Tip

The Office Assistant shown in the figure above is part of the Excel help facility and will be discussed in detail later in this Lesson.

Exploring the Excel Screen

Concept

In order to begin building a spreadsheet it is necessary to become familiar with the Excel window and worksheet elements.

Do It!

To familiarize herself with the Excel screen, Kay will click on various elements of the window.

1 Click the Maximize button ▣, located at the right side of the title bar, to enlarge the Excel window so that it fills your entire screen. The title bar at the top of the Excel window displays the name of the program and the title of the current worksheet that is open. When Excel opens, it automatically creates a new, empty worksheet file called Book1. The title bar also houses the Minimize ▬, Maximize ▣ or Restore ▣, and Close buttons ▣ used to resize the window. The Minimize button reduces the window to its program button on the taskbar. The Maximize button will appear if the Excel window has not been enlarged to fill the entire screen, and the Restore button, which returns the window to its previous size and location, will appear if the window is maximized. Double-clicking the title bar will also maximize or restore a window.

2 Click File to open the File menu, then guide the pointer over each menu to familiarize yourself with the different commands. The main menu bar is usually displayed right below the title bar. The menu bar contains lists with most of Excel's commands. Each word in the menu bar can be clicked to open a pull-down menu of commands. Or, a menu may be opened by pressing the Alt key and the underlined letter in the menu name. The menu bar also contains a set of sizing buttons. These controls function in the same manner as the application sizing buttons, only they apply to the active workbook window, not the entire Excel program. You can have more than one workbook window open in the Excel program window.

3 Move the pointer over the New button ▣. A brief description of the button's function, a ScreenTip, will appear in a small rectangle below the button. Guide the pointer over the toolbars, pausing on each button to read its description, as shown in **Figure 1-5**. The two rows of icons beneath the menu bar are called toolbars. Toolbar buttons provide shortcuts to many of Excel's most commonly used commands. You can customize the toolbars to contain the tools that you use most often. The top toolbar in **Figure 1-5** is called the Standard toolbar, and the lower toolbar is called the Formatting toolbar.

4 Click the Select All button, the gray rectangle in the upper-left corner of the worksheet where the row and column headings meet. The entire worksheet becomes highlighted, and the row and column heading buttons will become depressed. The worksheet is where you enter data to create your spreadsheet. A spreadsheet can contain many worksheets, and together multiple worksheets make up a workbook.

More

The Standard toolbar and Formatting toolbar are just two of the many toolbars available in Excel. To view and activate additional toolbars, open the View menu from the menu bar and highlight the Toolbars command. A submenu of toolbar names will appear. Click a toolbar to activate it. Excel toolbars are flexible objects. You can anchor them to any side of the Excel window by clicking and dragging, or float them over the middle of the Excel screen. If all the buttons associated with a particular toolbar do not fit on the toolbar due to window or screen size, a small arrow button will appear at the end of the toolbar. Click on the arrow to reveal a menu of the remaining buttons.

You may have noticed that the Excel window contains two sets of sizing buttons. The top set, in the window's title bar, controls the Excel application window. The bottom set controls the active Excel document.

Excel 2000

Figure 1-5 Elements of the Excel application window

Title bar

Menu bar

Standard toolbar

Formatting toolbar

Select All button

Cell pointer

Sizing buttons

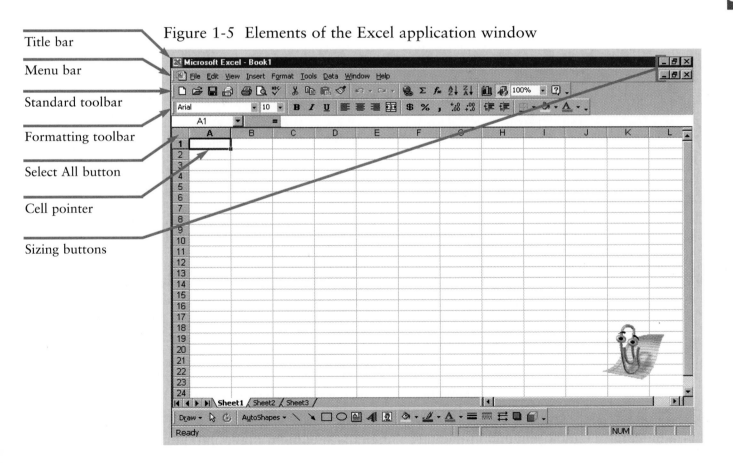

Exploring the Excel Screen (continued)

Do It!

5 Click the letter A that heads the first column. Column A becomes highlighted, as shown in **Figure 1-6**. The columns are designated by letters, from A to Z, then AA to AZ and so on up to IV, altogether making 256 columns.

6 Click the number 1 at the left of the first row. Row 1 becomes highlighted. The rows are labeled numerically down the left side of the worksheet, from 1 to 65,536.

7 Click the intersection of column D and row 7. Cell D7 is now active. Excel designates the active cell on the worksheet by bordering it with a dark rectangle called a cell pointer. Rows intersect with columns forming the grid system. Each intersection of a row and a column is called a cell. Cells are identified by an address composed of the letter and number of the column and row that intersect to form the cell. When a cell is active, you can enter new data into it or edit any data that is already there. You can make another cell active by clicking it, or by moving the cell pointer with the arrow keys found on the keyboard.

8 Click cell H9. Below the second row of icons are the name box and the formula bar. The name box displays the active cell address, H9, and the formula bar displays the data that you are working on, along with its location on the worksheet. The formula bar is now blank.

9 Double-click cell H9. At the bottom of the Excel screen is the status bar, which changes in response to the task in progress. As Figure 1-7 shows, "Enter" should now appear in the status bar indicating that you can enter a label, data, or a formula into the cell. The left side of this bar displays a brief description of Excel's current activities. The boxes to the right indicate the status of particular keys, such as the Caps Lock key.

10 Click the down arrow on the vertical scroll bar to move the spreadsheet down one row, hiding row 1. The vertical scroll bar on the far right side of the worksheet window and the horizontal scroll bar on the lower edge of the worksheet window help you move quickly around the worksheet.

11 Below the active worksheet, Excel provides Sheet tabs that you can click to switch to other worksheets in the open workbook. Click the Sheet 2 tab. Notice that the cell pointer moved from H9, the active cell on Sheet 1, to cell A1, the active cell on Sheet 2. Related worksheets can be arranged together in workbooks. Book 1 in the title bar actually stands for Workbook 1. Workbooks can contain up to 255 worksheets. Sheet tab scrolling buttons (in the lower-left corner of the window) help you view worksheet tabs not in the window.

Figure 1-6 Selecting a column

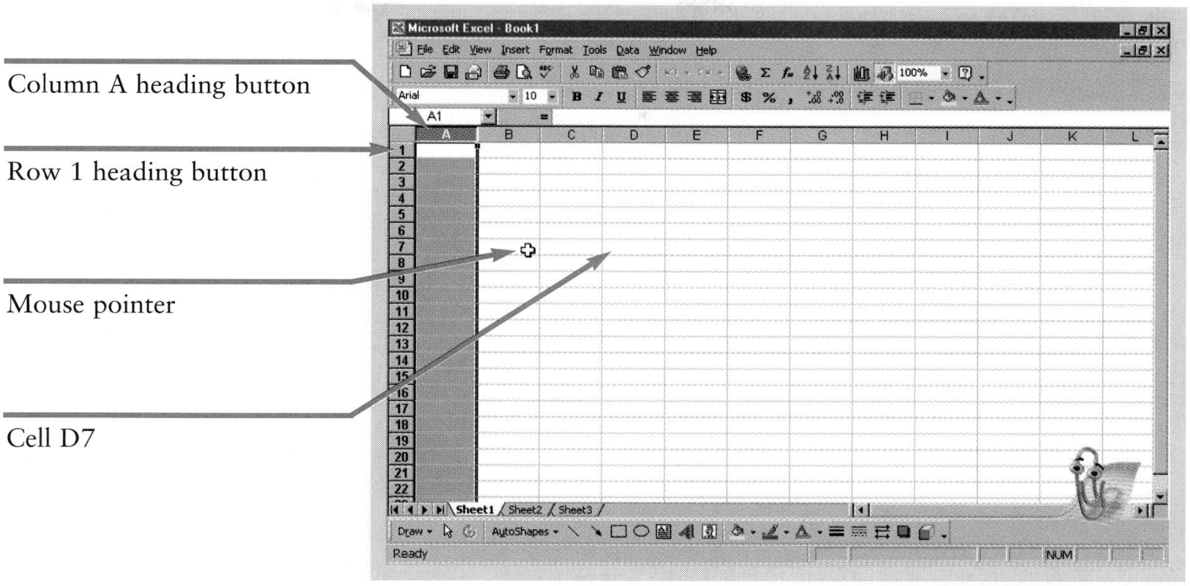

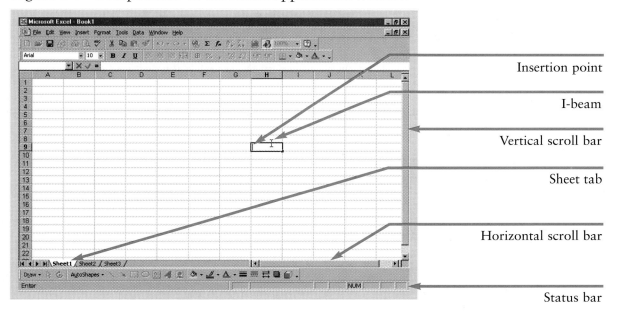

Column A heading button

Row 1 heading button

Mouse pointer

Cell D7

Excel 2000

Figure 1-7 Components of the Excel application window

Insertion point

I-beam

Vertical scroll bar

Sheet tab

Horizontal scroll bar

Status bar

Practice

To practice what you have learned in this Skill, click the Minimize button on the menu bar to minimize the document window and display it as a small title bar at the bottom of the window. Then click its Maximize button to enlarge the document.

Hot Tip

The document and application control menu icons, at the left end of the menu and title bars respectively, offer menus containing the Close and sizing commands.

Moving Around the Worksheet

Concept

To effectively use Excel you must be able to maneuver between cells in the work-space. To do this you may either use the mouse or the keyboard, depending on your personal preference or your current activity. For example, if you are entering a large quantity of data quickly into cells that are close together, it may be easier and more efficient to use the keyboard. If you need to select a cell that is far from the active cell, using the mouse would probably be more effective.

Do It!

Kay moves to various points on the Excel worksheet to familiarize herself with Excel's navigation.

1. Using the mouse, move the mouse pointer ✛ to cell B4 and click the left mouse button. The cell becomes highlighted, marking it as the active cell.

2. Press [←]. The cell pointer moves over one cell to the left to A4.

3. Press [↑]. The cell pointer moves up one cell to A3.

4. Press the [→], then [↓] to return the cell pointer to cell B4.

5. Click once on the arrow at the right end of the horizontal scroll bar. The worksheet will scroll right by one column.

6. Scroll down one row by clicking once on the arrow at the bottom vertical scroll bar.

7. Click the horizontal scroll bar arrow until column Z is visible. Notice that the scroll bar box shrinks to allow you a larger movement area, as seen in **Figure 1-8**.

8. Click and hold the mouse button on the horizontal scroll bar box. You have now grabbed the box. Drag the box to the left until you can see column A.

Figure 1-8 Getting around the Excel application window

Name box displays selected cell, B4, even though it is not currently visible

Row 4 button bold, indicating that a cell in that row is selected

Column names extend past Z and begin again with AA, AB, etc.

Horizontal scroll bar box

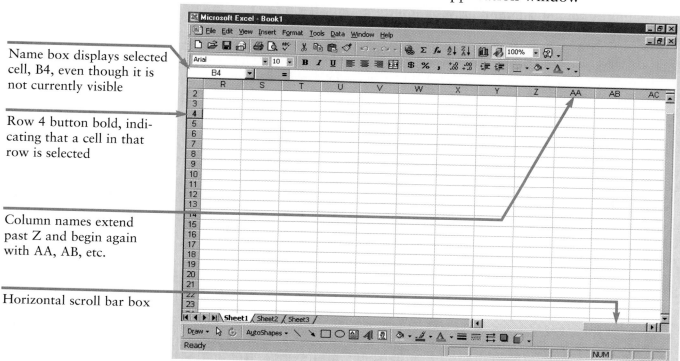

Excel 2000

Moving Around the Worksheet (continued)

Do It!

9 Click Edit, then select Go To. The Go To dialog box, shown in **Figure 1-9**, appears. The Go To command is useful when you have to move a great distance across the worksheet.

10 At the bottom of the dialog box there is a text box, the white area with a flashing insertion point, labeled Reference. Type Y95 in the Reference text box.

11 Click [Open]. Excel's cell pointer highlights cell Y95 in the worksheet.

12 Press [Ctrl]+[Home]. The cell pointer will jump to cell A1. The [Ctrl]+[Home] command is helpful for returning to the beginning of a worksheet.

More

At the bottom of the worksheet are three tabs labeled Sheet1, Sheet2, and Sheet3. A workbook is often made up of many worksheets, and each tab corresponds to a different worksheet. Interrelated data can be kept across multiple worksheets of the same workbook for viewing, cross referencing, and calculation. To go to a different worksheet, simply click its tab at the bottom of the window. New worksheets can be added to a workbook by using the Worksheet command on the Insert menu. The new worksheet will appear before the active worksheet. You can move a worksheet to a different place in the worksheet hierarchy by dragging its tab to the desired place in the row of tabs. The mouse pointer will appear with a blank sheet attached to it and a small arrow will indicate where the worksheet will be placed when you release the mouse button. The tab scrolling buttons, located to the left of the sheet tabs, allow you to view tabs that do not fit in the window. Clicking one of the outer buttons moves you to the beginning or end of the list of tabs, while clicking one of the inner buttons will move you through the tabs one at a time. If you right-click the tab scrolling buttons, a pop-up menu listing all of the tabs in your workbook will appear, allowing you to select a specific tab to jump to. Tabs can be renamed by double-clicking the tab to select its text, and then editing it like normal text. Right-clicking a tab opens a shortcut pop-up menu with commands that allow you to rename, delete, insert, and copy or move a worksheet.

Table 1-1 Moving in a Worksheet

MOVEMENT	ACTION
Left one cell	Press [←] or [Shift]+[Tab]
Right one cell	Press [→] or [Tab]
Up one cell	Press [↑] or [Shift]+[Enter]
Down one cell	Press [↓] or [Enter]
Left one column or right one column	Click the left arrow or right arrow on the horizontal scroll bar
Up one row or down one row	Click the up arrow or down arrow on the vertical scroll bar.
Up one screen or down one screen	Press [Page Up] or [Page Down]
Left one screen or right one screen	Press [Alt]+[Page Up] or [Alt]+[Page Down]
Go to cell A1	[Ctrl]+[Home]
Go to colum A in current row	[Home]

Excel 2000

Figure 1-9 Go To dialog box

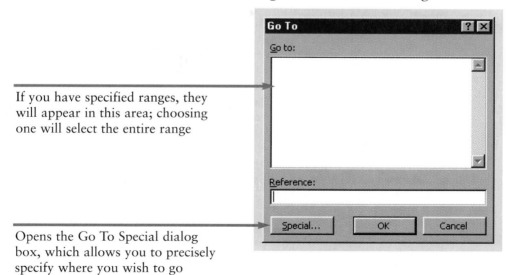

If you have specified ranges, they will appear in this area; choosing one will select the entire range

Opens the Go To Special dialog box, which allows you to precisely specify where you wish to go

Practice

Click cell E12 to make it active, then use the arrow keys to move the cell pointer to cell G7. Open the Go To dialog box and navigate to cell CT2041. Finally, position the cell pointer in cell A1.

Hot Tip

To move across a large area of blank cells press [End], the word END will appear in the status bar, then press an arrow key. The cell pointer will jump to the next filled cell in the direction of the arrow key pressed.

Entering Labels

Concept

Labels are used to annotate and describe the data you place into rows and columns. Properly labeled data makes your spreadsheet easy to understand and interpret. Labels can consist of text or numbers and are aligned left so as to differentiate them from data used in calculations. Excel automatically left-justifies labels. Labels should be entered into your spreadsheet first so that your rows and columns are defined before your begin to enter the calculable data.

Do It!

Kay enters the documentation and row labels for her spreadsheet.

1 Click cell A2 to make it the active cell. The address A2 appears in the name box.

2 Type Income and Expenditures for Kay's Hound Accessories, then click the Enter button ☑. The label will appear in the formula bar as you type. Even though the label is longer than the cell width, it will be displayed in its entirety as long as the next cell remains empty.

3 Click cell A3 and type File name: Profit1.xls, then press [Enter]. The label will be entered and the cell pointer will move down one row to cell A4.

4 Type Author: Kay Samoy, click cell D4 and type Date: 4/6/00. In cell A5 type Ranges:, in cell D5 type Macros:, and in cell F5 type Assumptions: Sales Growth. These labels are the documentation for your spreadsheet. Documentation describes and titles your spreadsheet. It contains the purpose, file name and author of the spreadsheet, the date it was created, as well as defining any ranges, macros and assumptions that it may contain.

5 Click cell A8 to make it the active cell. Type Income and then press [Enter]. The next six labels will be the row headings.

6 Type Sales, then press [Enter]; skip a cell and in cell A11 type Expenditures, then press [Enter]; in cell A12 type Rent, then press [Enter]; in cell A13 type Salaries, then press [Enter]; in cell A14 type Misc., then press [Enter]; and in cell A15 type Total Expenses, then press [Enter]. Your worksheet should now look like the one shown in Figure 1-10.

More

Then Enter button on the formula bar functions in much the same way as the Enter key on the keyboard, but after you click the Enter button, the cell pointer remains in the current cell instead of moving to the cell beneath. The Enter button disappears after you use it, but you can bring it back by clicking the text box on the formula bar. The Cancel button ☒ not only removes the contents from a cell, but also restores the cell's previous contents, if there were any.

Excel automatically assumes that a number is a value and aligns it to the right by default. If you wish to use a number as a label, simply type an apostrophe ['] before the number. The data will then be aligned to the left. The apostrophe will be hidden in the cell, but will be shown in the formula bar.

Figure 1-10 Entering labels

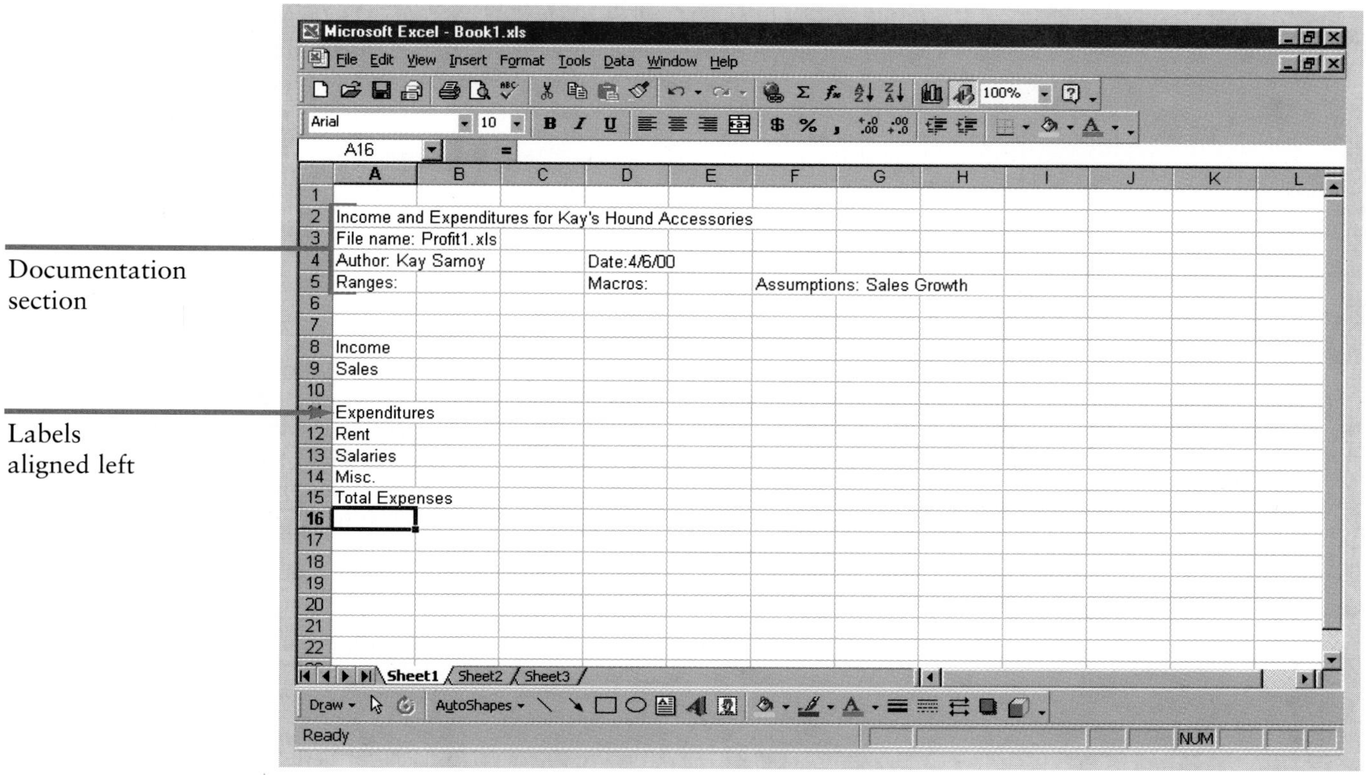

Documentation
section

Labels
aligned left

Practice

Click the **New** button 🗋 to open a new workbook. Beginning in cell A2, enter the following information as cell labels, pressing **[Enter]** after each: your name, today's date, your instructor's name, and the title of this course.

Hot Tip

If you start to enter a label whose first few letters match those of an adjacent cell in the column, Excel will automatically complete the label to match. If you do not wish to accept the suggestion, simply continue typing to overwrite Excel's suggestion.

Saving and Closing a Worksheet

Concept

Saving your work is important; if not saved, work can be lost due to power or computer failure. Once a file has been saved, it can be reopened at any time for editing or viewing. Your workbook can be saved to a hard drive, floppy disk, network drive, or even a Web server. Closing a file removes it from the screen and puts it away for later use. You can close a file while leaving the application open for use with other Excel files. Or, if you are finished using Excel, you can exit the application.

Do It!

Kay wants to save her worksheet under the name Profit1 in a folder titled Kay's Hound Accessories.

1. Click Window, then select Book1.xls from the menu if it is not already active. Book1.xls will become the active document.

2. Click File, then click Save As. Notice that the Save As command is followed by an ellipsis (three dots), indicating that a dialog box will open when the command is executed. The Save As dialog box opens, as shown in **Figure 1-11**. (If you had chosen the Save command, the Save As dialog would have appeared anyway, as this is the first time you will be saving your document.) The file name Book1.xls automatically appears highlighted in the File Name text box, ready to be changed.

3. To give the workbook file a more distinctive name, type Profit1. The .xls file extension will automatically be added. As you type the name, Book1.xls will be overwritten. Windows 95 and 98 support file names of up to 255 characters. The file name can contain uppercase or lowercase letters, numbers, and most symbols.

4. Click the Save in list arrow to choose where to save the file. Excel is programmed to save newly created files in the My Documents folder by default. Click 3½ Floppy (A:) if your student files will be stored on a floppy disk or Maindisk (C:) if your student files are to be stored on your hard drive. Consult your instructor if you have any doubts about this matter.

5. Click the Create New Folder button . The New Folder dialog box will appear with the folder name New Folder highlighted in the Name: text box, as shown in **Figure 1-12**.

Figure 1-11 Save As dialog box

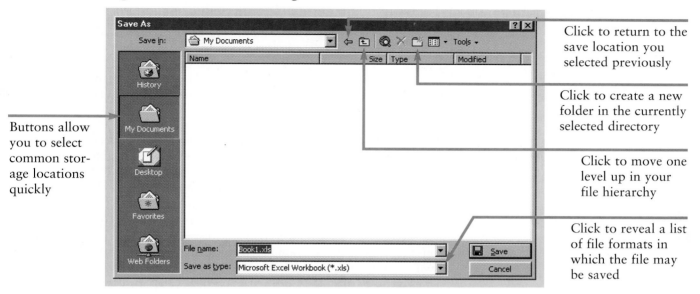

Buttons allow you to select common storage locations quickly

Click to return to the save location you selected previously

Click to create a new folder in the currently selected directory

Click to move one level up in your file hierarchy

Click to reveal a list of file formats in which the file may be saved

Excel 2000

Figure 1-12 New Folder dialog box

Future location of folder being created

Saving and Closing a Worksheet (continued)

Do It!

6 Type Kay's Hound Accessories. The default name will be replaced with the new text.

7 Click [OK]. The new folder will be created and opened automatically in the Save As dialog box. The contents window will be blank since there are no files or folders in Kay's folder, as shown in **Figure 1-13**.

8 Click [💾 Save] to store the worksheet in Kay's folder. The Save As dialog box will close and the new file name will appear in the Excel window's title bar.

9 Click File, then click Close. The workbook file is removed from the Excel window.

More

You can also use the AutoSave option to have Excel automatically save your file every few minutes. The AutoSave command is found on the Tools menu. If it is not there, you will have to install the AutoSave add-in. Select the Add-Ins command from the Tools menu to open the Add-Ins dialog box. Click the check box next to AutoSave, and then click the OK button. After Excel has set up the AutoSave feature, select it from the Tools menu; the AutoSave dialog box, shown in **Figure 1-14**, will open. You can turn AutoSave on or off with the check box at the top-left of the dialog box, and you can choose the time between saves by entering an interval in the text box labeled minutes. You have the option of saving just the active workbook or all of the open workbooks, and Excel can prompt you before it auto saves if you wish, so as to avoid inadvertently saving unwanted changes.

Understanding the difference between the Save command and the Save As command is an important part of working with most software. When you save a new file for the first time, the two commands function identically; they both open the Save As dialog box, allowing you to choose a name and storage location for the file. Once you have saved a file, the commands serve different purposes. Choosing the Save command will update the original file with any changes you have made, maintaining the same file name and location. Choosing the Save As command will permit you to save a different version of the same file, with a new name, location, or both.

Figure 1-13 Saving a file in a new folder

New folder
selected in
Save in: box

Default file name
given by Excel

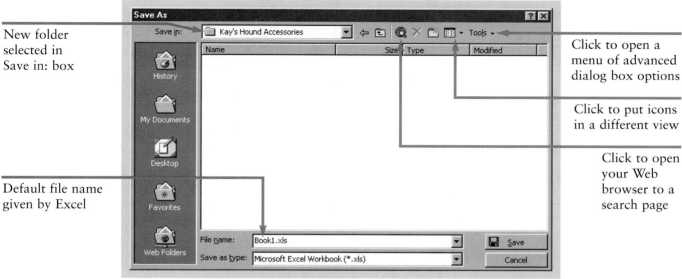

Click to open a
menu of advanced
dialog box options

Click to put icons
in a different view

Click to open
your Web
browser to a
search page

Excel 2000

Figure 1-14 AutoSave dialog box

Use this check box
to turn AutoSave
on or off

Check here to require
confirmation before
AutoSave operates

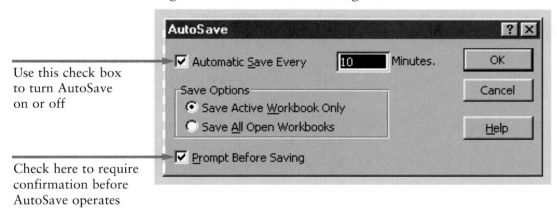

Practice

Save the workbook you created in the
Practice for the previous Skill on your student disk as Practice1-7 and then close the
workbook.

Hot Tip

The Save button 🖫 on the Standard toolbar and the keyboard combination [Ctrl]+[S]
are shortcuts to the Save command.

EX 1.19

Opening a Worksheet

Concept

In order to work with a saved file you must first open it. Opening a file requires that you know the file's name and the location in which it is stored.

Do It!

Kay needs to open her file so that she can edit one of the labels.

1 Click File, then click Open. Notice that the Open command is followed by an ellipsis (three dots) indicating that a dialog box will open, as the command requires more information. The Open dialog box will appear as shown in **Figure 1-15**.

2 Earlier you saved the file Profit1 in a folder named Kay's Hound Accessories. Click the Look in drop down list arrow and select the drive where your student files are stored. Insert your Student Disk into the A: drive and click the 3½ Floppy (A:) if they are stored on a floppy, or click Maindisk (C:) if they are in a folder on your hard disk. A list of the files and folders on the drive will appear in the list box.

3 Click the folder named Kay's Hound Accessories to select it, and then click the Open button 🗁 Open ▾ . The files housed in the folder will appear in the contents window.

4 Double-click the Profit1 file. The Open dialog box disappears and the worksheet will be displayed in the Excel window. Notice that the cell pointer is in the same cell it was in when you last saved the worksheet.

More

If you cannot remember the name of storage location of a particular file that you need to open, Excel provides a powerful search facility that can help you. Click the Tools button in the Open dialog box and then choose the Find command from the menu that appears as shown in **Figure 1-16**. The Find dialog box, shown in **Figure 1-17**, will open. From the Find dialog box, you can search any drive or folder accessible from your computer for a file. You can conduct your search using a wide variety of properties including file name, the date the file was last modified, or even the name of the person who created it. Each property has its own set of conditions that you can apply to the search. For example, the File name property allows you to find a file whose name includes, begins with, or ends with a specific character or combination of characters. You submit this value in the Value text-entry box. Use the selection and text-entry boxes at the bottom of the dialog box to set your criteria, and then click the Find Now button to initiate the search. If your search is successful, the file you requested will be selected in the Open dialog box. Once you have run a successful search, you can save it in case you ever need to locate that file again.

The Open button in the Open dialog box includes an arrow on its right edge. Clicking this arrow opens a menu that provides commands for opening a file in a number of different ways. For example, the Open Read-Only command permits you to view a file, but prohibits you from saving changes to it. The Open Copy command creates a copy of the file you are opening and opens the copy instead. The Open in Browser command opens HTML files in your Web browser rather than in Excel.

Figure 1-15 Open dialog box

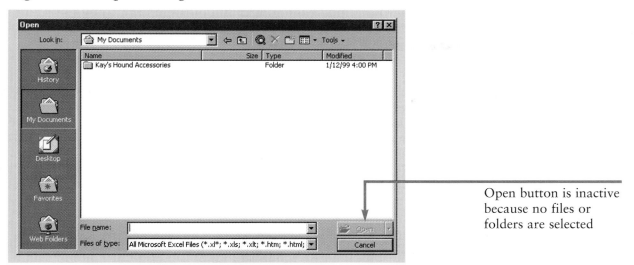

Open button is inactive because no files or folders are selected

Excel 2000

Figure 1-16 Find command

Figure 1-17 Find dialog box

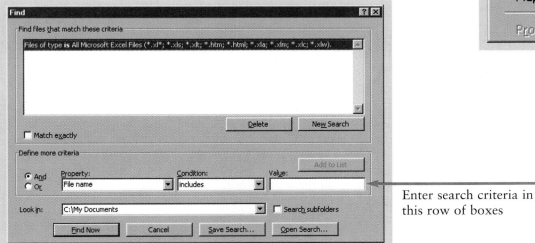

Enter search criteria in this row of boxes

Practice

To practice opening Excel documents, open the student file **Practice-Lesson 1.xls**. Then save it to your student disk as **MyPractice 1**.

Hot Tip

When conducting a file search, activate the Search subfolders check box to ensure that you the search includes all folders in a particular location on just the top-level of the folder or drive you selected.

Editing a Cell's Information

Concept

Many spreadsheet documents are used over a long period of time and undergo constant updating. Information entered into a cell is not permanent. You can change, or edit, the contents of cell at any time. Editing the contents of a cell is very similar to editing text in a word processing document.

Do It!

Kay wants to edit cell A11 to change Expenditures to Expenses.

1. Click cell A11. The cell pointer moves to cell A11 and Expenditures is displayed in the formula bar.

2. Move the mouse pointer from the worksheet to the formula bar and position it between the n and the d of the word Expenditures (the pointer will change from a cross ✚ to an I-beam I) and click. A blinking insertion point will appear, the formula bar buttons will be displayed, and the mode indicator on the status bar will read Edit, as shown in **Figure 1-18**.

3. Click and hold the left mouse button, then drag the I-beam to the right, over the last seven letters of the word Expenditures. The rest of the formula bar will become highlighted. Highlighting, or selecting, text allows it to be edited.

4. Type **ses** and then click the Enter button ✔. The new text will replace the incorrect label and the spreadsheet will look like **Figure 1-19**.

5. Save your workbook by clicking the Save button 🖫.

More

Excel provides you with multiple ways to edit a cell's information. You can select the cell you wish to edit and then click the formula bar, as described above. You may also double-click a desired cell, making a flashing insertion point appear. Then you can use the backspace and/or delete keys to remove the character to the left or right of the insertion point respectively, and enter new characters to edit the cell. Or, you can double-click a second time to highlight all of the cell's contents and edit the selection. Finally, you can select a cell and then press [F2], again making the insertion point appear in the selected cell.

Figure 1-18 Editing a cell label

Place the insertion point with the mouse

Contents of the selected cell appear above in the formula bar

Indicates that Excel is in edit mode, allowing you to change the contents of the selected cell

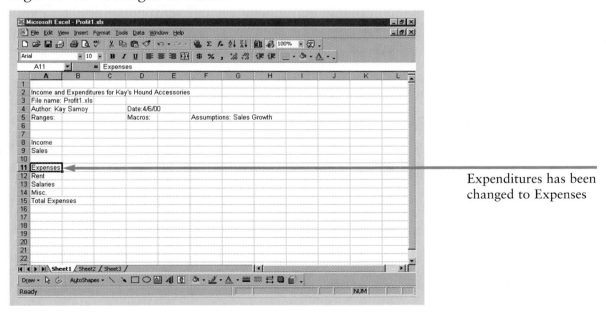

Figure 1-19 Changed cell label

Expenditures has been changed to Expenses

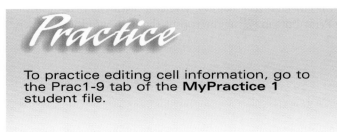

Practice

To practice editing cell information, go to the Prac1-9 tab of the **MyPractice 1** student file.

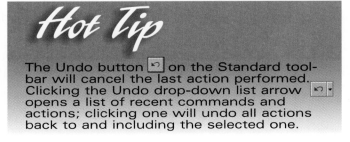

Hot Tip

The Undo button ⟲ on the Standard toolbar will cancel the last action performed. Clicking the Undo drop-down list arrow ⟲▾ opens a list of recent commands and actions; clicking one will undo all actions back to and including the selected one.

Excel 2000

Using the Office Assistant

Concept

Even the most experienced computer users need help from time to time. The Office Assistant provides several methods for getting help in Excel. You can choose from a list of topics that the Assistant suggests based on the most recent functions you have performed. You can also view tips related to your current activity. Or, you can ask a question in plain English. The Office Assistant will reply with several help topics related to your question.

Do It!

Kay has a question about the Office Assistant. She will use the Office Assistant to get help.

1. If the Office Assistant is not active, click ⃞ on the Standard toolbar. The Assistant and its dialog balloon appear asking what you would like to do. Click the text box that reads Type your question here, and then click Search. The text will be replaced by an insertion point.

2. In the text box, type How do I hide the Office Assistant? and then click Search . A list of topics appears in the balloon, as shown in **Figure 1-20**.

3. Click the first topic, Show, hide, or turn off the Office Assistant. **Figure 1-21** shows the Microsoft Excel Help window that appears.

4. Read the Help topic pertaining to the Office Assistant.

5. When you have finished reading about the Office Assistant's capabilities, click the Close ✕ button in the upper-right corner of the window.

More

From time to time the Assistant will offer you tips on how to use Excel more efficiently. The appearance of a small light bulb, either next to the Assistant or on the Office Assistant button, indicates that there is a tip to be viewed. To see the tip, click the light bulb in whichever location it appears.

The Office Assistant can be customized. Click the Options button in its dialog balloon to open the Office Assistant dialog box. This dialog box has two tabs: Gallery and Options. The Gallery tab contains different assistant characters you can install, and scrolling through the characters provides you with a preview of each one. From the Options tab, shown in **Figure 1-22**, you can control the Assistant's behavior and capabilities, and decide what kinds of tips it will show. You can also access Office Assistant commands by right-clicking the Assistant itself.

If your computer is properly connected to a printer, you can print the text of any help topic. Simply click the Print button 🖨 at the top of the help window to open the Print dialog box.

Figure 1-20 Assistant's search results

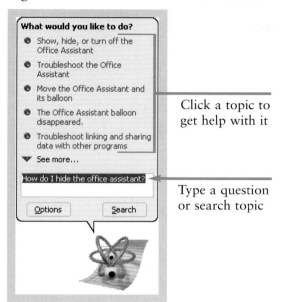

Click a topic to get help with it

Type a question or search topic

Figure 1-21 Help with the Office Assistant

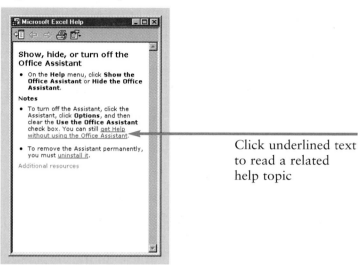

Click underlined text to read a related help topic

Excel 2000

Figure 1-22 Office Assistant dialog box

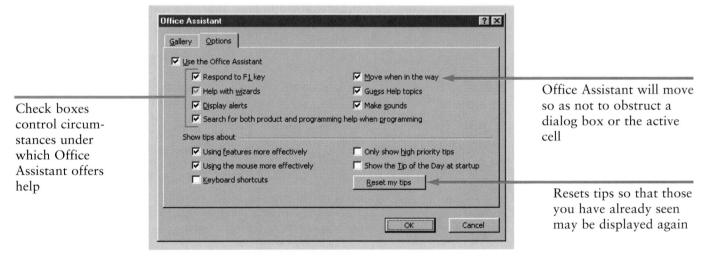

Check boxes control circumstances under which Office Assistant offers help

Office Assistant will move so as not to obstruct a dialog box or the active cell

Resets tips so that those you have already seen may be displayed again

Practice

Use the Office Assistant to learn about moving the Office Assistant and its balloon.

Hot Tip

The Office Assistant is common to all Office 2000 applications. Therefore, any Assistant options you change will affect it in all Office programs.

 # Other Excel Help Features

Concept

Working with new software can be confusing, and, at times, even intimidating. Fortunately, Microsoft Excel offers a number of built-in help features in addition to the Office Assistant that you can use when you encounter problems or just have a question about a particular aspect of the program. The What's This? command and the Help tabs are two such features.

Do It!

Kay will use the What's This? command to get more information about the Name Box, and the Help tabs to find out more about keyboard shortcuts.

1   Click Help on the menu bar, then click What's This?. A question mark will be added to the mouse pointer ▷?. With this pointer, you can click many Excel features to receive a ScreenTip that explains them.

2   Click the Name Box. A ScreenTip like the one in **Figure 1-23** will appear to explain the item you clicked. Read the tip, and then click the mouse to erase it.

3   Click the Office Assistant (activate the feature from the Help menu first, if necessary). Click any help topic or tip the Assistant is currently offering.

4   When the Help window for that topic appears, click the Show button ◁▣ . The window will expand to a two-paneled format. The left panel consists of three tabs while the right panel is used to display selected help files.

5   Click the Index tab to bring it to the front of the panel if it is not already there.

6   Click in the text-entry box labeled Type keywords:, and then type keyboard. Notice that the list box in the middle of the tab scrolls automatically to match your entry.

7   When you see the word keyboard appear in the list box, double-click it. After a moment, the help topics related to keyboard will be displayed in the box at the bottom of the tab.

8   Find Keyboard shortcuts in the Choose a topic list box (you may have to scroll down) and click it. The Keyboard shortcuts help file will be loaded into the right panel of the window as shown in **Figure 1-24**.

9   Close the Help window when you finish working with it.

More

The Index tab of the Help Topics dialog box is very helpful if you know what the task you are trying to accomplish is called, or if you know the name of the feature that you want to explore. If you are unsure of exactly what you are looking for, the Contents tab may be a better option for you. The Contents tab contains every Help topic that Excel offers, broken down by category, and is useful if you wish to obtain a broad view of the topics available. It is organized like an outline or the table of contents you might find in a book. It begins with general topics, symbolized by book icons, each of which can be expanded to reveal more specific and focused subtopics. Once you have revealed a general topic's subtopics, you can select a subtopic in the left panel to display it in the right panel, just as on the Index tab. The Answer Wizard tab replicates the Office Assistant, allowing you to request help topics by entering questions in your own words. Once you have clicked the Show button to display the Help tabs in a Help window, the button changes to the Hide button. Click the Hide button to collapse the window back to a single panel.

Excel 2000

Figure 1-23 Name Box What's This? ScreenTip

Name box

The box at the left end of the formula bar that identifies the selected cell, chart item, or drawing object. Type the name in the **Name** box, and then press ENTER to quickly name a selected cell or range. To move to and select a previously named cell, click its name in the **Name** box.

Figure 1-24 Using the Help tabs

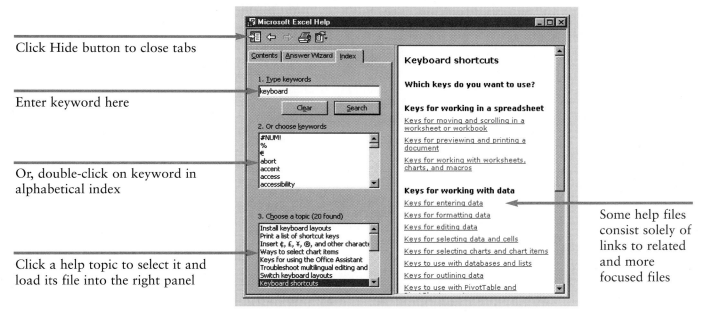

Click Hide button to close tabs

Enter keyword here

Or, double-click on keyword in alphabetical index

Click a help topic to select it and load its file into the right panel

Some help files consist solely of links to related and more focused files

Practice

Use the Index to find shortcut keys that relate to the Office Assistant.

Hot Tip

If your computer is connected to the Internet, you can access Microsoft's Web pages directly from Excel. Open the Help menu and click **Office on the Web** to launch your Web browser and go directly to the Office Web site.

Exiting Excel

Concept

It is important to exit the Excel program properly when you are finished with the day's work session. Closing the application correctly will help you avoid data loss.

Do It!

Kay has finished using Excel for the day and is ready to exit the application.

1. Click File, then click Close. Since you have altered the spreadsheet since the last time you saved, a dialog box will open asking if you want to save changes in Profit1.xls.

2. Click [Yes]. Excel will save the changes you have made and the worksheet will disappear from the window.

3. To close the application click File, then click Exit (see **Figure 1-25**). Excel closes and removes itself from the desktop.

More

There are other ways you can close a file and exit Excel. The easiest method is to use the Close buttons [X] located in the upper-right corner of the window. The Close button on the menu bar is for the active workbook, and the Close button on the title bar is for the application.

You may open any menu on the menu bar by pressing the [Alt] key followed by the underlined letter in the menu's title. You will notice that menu commands also have a letter in their name underlined; typing the underlined letter will activate its command on the open menu. For example, with the File menu open, typing [c] will close the file and pressing [x] will exit Excel. If you have more than one workbook open in Excel, the program will allow you to save changes to all of them at once before closing.

Figure 1-25 Closing the Excel application

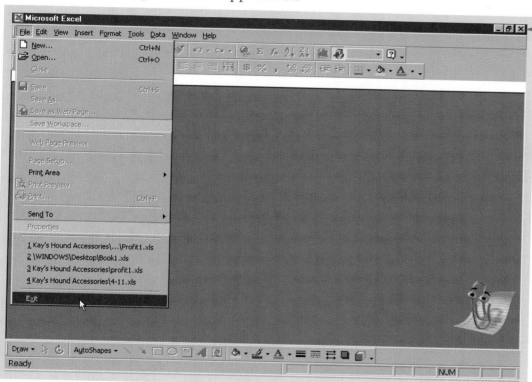

Clicking this Close button will likewise exit the application

Excel 2000

Practice

Open Excel, and then Exit the application by clicking the Close button [X] on the title bar.

Hot Tip

Pressing the [Ctrl] key plus [W] will close your file, while [Alt] + [F4] is the key combination used to exit Excel.

Shortcuts

Function	Button/Mouse	Menu	Keyboard
Create a new file	🗋	Click File, then click New	[Ctrl]+[N]
Open a file	📂	Click File, then click Open	[Ctrl]+[O]
Maximize a window	◻	Click Control icon, then click Maximize	
Minimize a window	_	Click Control icon, then click Minimize	
Restore a window	⧉	Click Control icon, then click Restore	
Close a window	✕	Click Control icon, then click Close	[Alt]+[F4] (application) [Ctrl]+[W] (document)
Confirm a cell entry	✓		[Enter], [Tab], Arrow keys
Cancel a cell entry	✕	Click Edit, then click Undo typing	[Ctrl]+[Z]
Search the Web (from the Open dialog box)	🔍		
Save a file	💾	Click File, then click Save	[Ctrl]+[S]
Office Assistant	❓	Click Help, then click Microsoft Excel Help	[F1]
What's This?	❓ In a dialog box	Click Help, then click What's This?	[Shift]+[F1]

Identify Key Features

Name the items identified by callouts in **Figure 1-26**.

Figure 1-26 Elements of the Excel screen

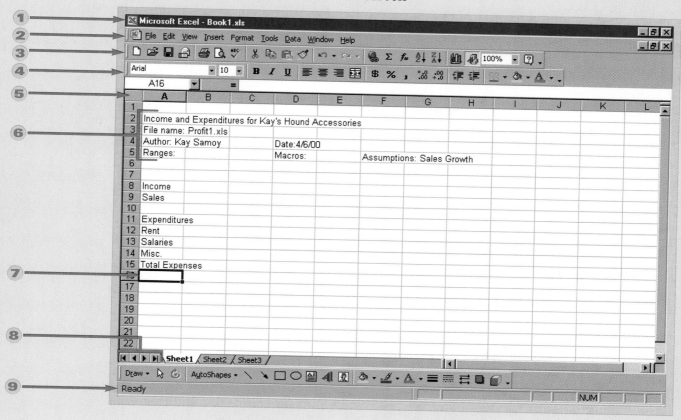

Excel 2000

Select The Best Answer

10. Click this to make the Excel window fill the screen

11. Displays the active cell address

12. Displays a brief description of your current activities in Excel

13. Allows you to choose a name and location for storing a file

14. Saves your file keeping its current name and location

15. Answers your questions and offers guidance as you work

16. Allows you to search for a file from the Open dialog box

17. Location where you can edit the contents of a cell

a. Name Box

b. Office Assistant

c. Maximize button

d. Find command

e. Save As command

f. Formula bar

g. Save button

h. Status bar

Quiz (continued)

Complete the Statement

18. To select an entire column, click:

    a. The first cell in the column

    b. Any cell in the column

    c. Its letter column heading

    d. The corresponding row number

19. Text or numbers that describe your data are called:

    a. Annotations

    b. Ranges

    c. Justifications

    d. Labels

20. Pressing [Ctrl]+[Home] will:

    a. Move your view up one screen

    b. Move your view down one screen

    c. Move the cell pointer to cell A1

    d. Move the cell pointer to Column A in the current row

21. All of the following actions will move the cell pointer to another cell except:

    a. Clicking the Enter button

    b. Pressing the Enter key

    c. Pressing the Tab key

    d. Pressing an Arrow key

22. A well-designed spreadsheet does not require:

    a. Documentation

    b. Multiple worksheets

    c. Input

    d. Output

23. All of these are Excel Help features except:

    a. The Index tab

    b. The Office Assistant

    c. What's This?

    d. The HelpWizard

24. A file extension:

    a. Allows you to see a hidden file

    b. Lets you edit the information in a cell

    c. Associates a file with a specific application

    d. Is part of Excel's Help facility

25. A workbook can contain:

    a. 16 worksheets

    b. 255 worksheets

    c. 3 worksheets

    d. 65, 536 worksheets

26. Excel assumes that numbers entered on the worksheet are:

    a. Values

    b. Labels

    c. Formulas

    d. Apostrophes

Interactivity

Test Your Skills

1. Open the Excel application and document a new spreadsheet:

   a. Use the Start button to launch Microsoft Excel.

   b. Add a documentation section to the blank worksheet using the title Class Schedule, your name, and the date.

   c. When you document the file name, use the name Test 1.xls.

   d. Include labels for ranges and macros. Your documentation section should occupy Rows 1-4 of the worksheet.

2. Design a worksheet that displays your daily class schedule:

   a. Add labels in Row 6 for the days of the week. Start in cell B6, and skip a column between each day. Friday should be in cell J6.

   b. Add labels in Column A for your class periods. Enter the time of your earliest class in cell A8, and then add a label for each subsequent class period through your last class of the day. Skip a row between each time label.

   c. Enter the names of your classes in the appropriate cells where the day of the week and the time intersect.

3. Get help from the Office Assistant:

   a. Open the Office Assistant's dialog balloon.

   b. Ask the Assistant for information on how to customize toolbars.

   c. Choose a topic that the Assistant provides, and then read the information in the Help window.

   d. Close the Help window when you are done, and then close the Office Assistant's window.

4. Save your file and exit Excel:

   a. Save your spreadsheet under the name Test 1.xls.

   b. Exit Microsoft Excel.

Interactivity (continued)

Problem Solving

1. Create a new spreadsheet following the design principles you learned in Lesson 1. Design this spreadsheet to log your daily activities. Enter labels for the days of the week just as you did in the previous exercise, but this time add Saturday and Sunday after Friday, and do not leave a blank column between each day. Instead of class periods, add labels down Column A for Class, Activities, Meals, Studying/Homework, Leisure, and Sleep. Do not skip rows between labels. Save the file as Solved 1-1.xls.

2. Due to a recent merger, your accounting firm can now increase the budgets of several departments. You are elated to learn that you will have an additional $10,000 available for your expense account. As a member of the Human Resources department, you know how much this money will help you attract the top candidates for your company's job openings. Use Excel to design a spreadsheet that will detail your strategy for utilizing the new funds over the next year. You do not have to enter any monetary values yet. Simply set up the structure of the worksheet with labels. Save the file as Solved-HR.xls.

3. At your urging, the restaurant you manage has just purchased a new computer complete with Office 2000. The owner of the restaurant, who was reluctant to make the purchase, wants you to prove that it was a sound investment. Using Excel, design a spreadsheet that will allow you to keep track of the waitstaff's schedule over one week. Your worksheet should include columns for Time In and Time Out each day of the week. Save the file as Solved-Rest.xls.

L E S S O N

2

MANIPULATING DATA IN A WORKSHEET

O ne of the greatest advantages of using spreadsheet software is that it automates many of the processes that take up so much time when done by hand. In Excel, you can move or copy data from one location in a worksheet to another quickly and easily.

Excel also automates your calculations by using mathematical formulas. If you instruct Excel what operation to perform, and where to get the data, the program will execute the calculations for you. The Paste Function feature prevents you from having to enter complicated formulas that Excel already knows. Once you have entered a formula or a function, you can even paste it into a new location.

Often, businesses like to use the data they have gathered to make projections about their business. In Excel, you can use assumptions to perform calculations under different conditions, altering the results of the worksheet each time. This technique is known as What-if analysis, and takes full advantage of Excel's versatility.

CASE STUDY
In this lesson, Kay will use Excel's Cut, Copy, and Paste features to manipulate the labels in her spreadsheet. She will also fill out the worksheet with values, and then use those values to perform calculations using formulas and functions. Then she will change her output by performing a What-If analysis. Finally, Kay will print a copy of her worksheet.

 # Cutting, Copying, and Pasting Data

Concept

Excel makes it easy to transfer data from cell to cell. Cutting or Copying information places it on the Office Clipboard, a temporary storage place for data. If you have used the Windows operating system or previous versions of Microsoft Excel before, you may be familiar with the Windows Clipboard. The Office Clipboard can hold up to 12 items at once, while the Windows Clipboard holds only one. The two Clipboards are related in the following ways: the last item you sent to the Office Clipboard can also be found on the Windows Clipboard; when you clear the Office Clipboard the Windows Clipboard is erased as well. Both Clipboards are volatile. That is, they are erased automatically when you shut down your computer. The Paste command inserts the last item you sent to the Clipboard at the insertion point. Cell contents may also be moved by dragging and dropping with the mouse.

Do It!

Kay wants to add the column heading Quarter in four cells, B6, C6, D6, and E6 of her spreadsheet. Then she will cut and paste the column headings from row 6 to row 7.

1. Open Excel by clicking the Start button, then selecting Excel from the Programs menu. The Excel window will appear on your desktop.

2. Click the Open button 📂, then find the folder named Kay's Hound Accessories, and open Profit1.xls. Your workbook will appear in the Excel window.

3. Click cell B6. The cell pointer will appear in cell B6 to indicate it is active.

4. Type Quarter, then click the Enter button ✓ to confirm the entry. The label will appear in cell B6.

5. Click Edit, then click Copy to send a duplicate of the contents of the selected cell to the Clipboard. An animated dashed border appears around the copied selection, as shown in Figure 2-1.

6. Press [Tab] to move the cell pointer to cell C6. Notice that the animated border remains in cell B6.

7. Click Edit, then click Paste to insert the copied text into the selected cell.

8. Move the mouse pointer to the fill handle, the black square in the lower-right corner of the cell, until it changes to a crosshair ✛ indicating that the selection can be copied elsewhere in the document.

9. Click the left mouse button and drag the fill pointer to cell E6. The cells will appear with a gray border, identifying them as a possible destination for the copied data, and a ScreenTip displaying the text to be copied will appear, as seen in Figure 2-2.

10. Release the mouse button. A copy of the selected data will appear in cells D6 and E6.

Figure 2-1 Copying a cell

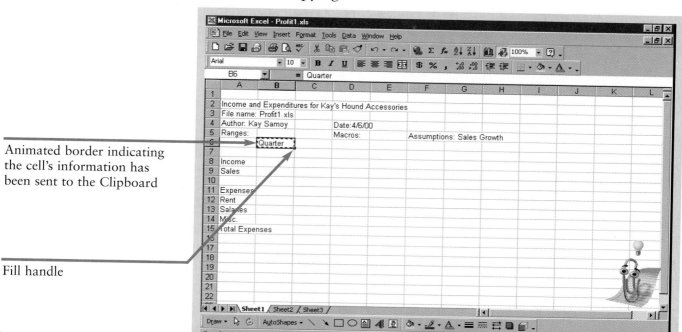

Animated border indicating the cell's information has been sent to the Clipboard

Fill handle

Excel 2000

Figure 2-2 Selected destination cells

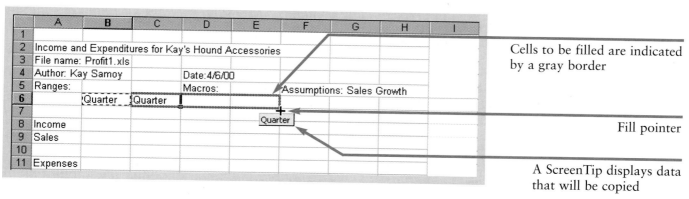

Cells to be filled are indicated by a gray border

Fill pointer

A ScreenTip displays data that will be copied

Cutting, Copying, and Pasting Data (continued)

Do It!

11 Double-click cell B6 to put it into edit mode. Edit will appear in the status bar.

12 Place the I-beam after Quarter, press [Space], then type [1]. The label will read Quarter 1.

13 Repeat the previous steps so that cells C6 through E6 read Quarter 2 thorough 4 respectively. Your worksheet should now resemble the one in **Figure 2-3**.

14 Click cell B6 to select it, then drag the mouse pointer to cell E6 so that all four cells are encompassed in the cell pointer. Cells C6, D6, and E6 will be highlighted.

15 Click the Cut button ✂ on the Standard toolbar. The column headings are surrounded by an animated border.

16 Click cell B7, then drag to cell E7 to select the entire group as the destination cells for the cut information.

17 Click the Paste button 📋. The column headings in row 6 will be pasted into row 7, as shown in **Figure 2-4**.

18 Save your worksheet by clicking the Save button 💾.

More

You can move or copy a cell's contents with the mouse by dragging and dropping. Dragging involves positioning the pointer over an object, clicking the left mouse button to grab the object, and then moving the mouse, and the object, to a new location. When the mouse pointer is over a cell pointer it will change to an arrow. You can then click and drag the cell pointer to a new location to move the contents of the selected cell or cells without having to use the Clipboard. Releasing the mouse button drops a grabbed object into place. Pressing [Ctrl] while dragging and dropping causes the pointer to change to the copy pointer. When dropped, the contents of the selection will appear in the new location but the original information will remain intact.

If you want to fill a range of cells with copies of a selected cell or cells, move the mouse pointer to the fill handle, the square at the bottom-right corner of a cell pointer, until it changes to a crosshair. Then click and drag the mouse pointer in the direction of the columns or rows that you wish to fill; a gray border will appear around the cells which will be filled with copies of your original selection when you release the mouse button. Using the fill handle allows you to make multiple copies of a selected cell or range's content at the same time, whereas you can only make a single copy of a cell or range's content using the drag-and-drop method described above.

As stated earlier, you can store up to 12 items on the Office Clipboard. To paste an item other than the one you cut or copied most recently, open the View menu, highlight Toolbars, and click Clipboard on the submenu that appears. The Clipboard toolbar, shown in **Figure 2-5**, will open. The Clipboard toolbar allows you to choose exactly which stored item you want to paste. Point to an icon on the toolbar to receive a ScreenTip that tells you what piece of data the icon represents.

Figure 2-3 Edited cells

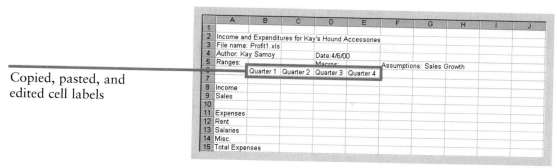

Copied, pasted, and
edited cell labels

Figure 2-4 Cut and pasted cells

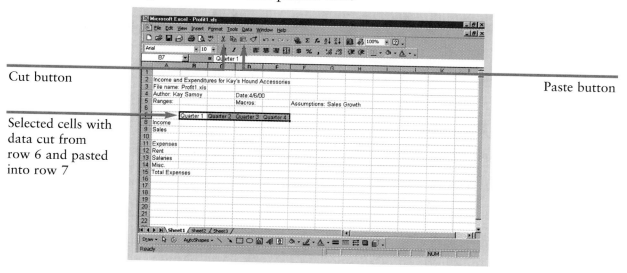

Cut button

Paste button

Selected cells with
data cut from
row 6 and pasted
into row 7

Excel 2000

Figure 2-5 Office Clipboard

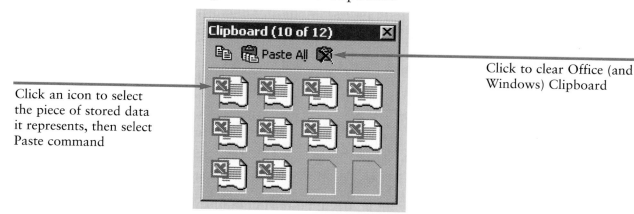

Click to clear Office (and
Windows) Clipboard

Click an icon to select
the piece of stored data
it represents, then select
Paste command

Practice

Open the practice file **Practice-Lesson 2.xls**, save it as **MyPractice2**, and then follow the instructions on the **Prac2-1** sheet.

Hot Tip

The Cut command removes the contents of a cell and sends them to the Clipboard. The Copy command sends a copy of a cell's content to the Clipboard, leaving the original data in the cell.

Entering Values

Concept

Values are numbers, formulas or functions that Excel uses in calculations. They must be entered and confirmed in the same way that labels are.

Do It!

Kay wants to enter sales and expense values into her worksheet.

1 Click cell B9 to make it the active cell.

2 Type 970000, then press [Tab]. The first quarter sales value is entered into the cell and the cell pointer moves to the right to cell C9.

3 Now enter the rest of the Sales values in the row, pressing [Tab] after each: 1000400, 1210305, 1484032.

4 Click cell B12 to activate it.

5 Type 45000 and then click the Enter button ☑.

6 Since the rent is the same for each quarter, copy the data in cell B12 and paste it into the other three cells in the row; C12, D12, and E12, by clicking on the fill handle, dragging it to cell E12, and then releasing it. Notice the ScreenTip that shows the data that will be copied.

7 Click cell B13 to activate it and enter the following four values into the Salaries row, pressing [Tab] after each: 30000, 30000, 51750, 61750.

8 Click cell B14 to activate it and enter the following four Misc. values into the row, pressing [Tab] after each: 10200, 8188, 7900, 9940. Your worksheet should now resemble the one shown in **Figure 2-6**.

More

You may have noticed that the values you entered, unlike labels, were aligned to the right when confirmed. Excel aligns values to the right by default and recognizes an entry as a value when it is a number or it is preceded by +, -, =, @, #, or $. Ordinals (1st, 2nd, 3rd etc.) and other combinations of numbers and letters are recognized as labels. Sometimes you may want to use a number, such as a year, as a label; in this case, you can type an apostrophe (') before it to make Excel recognize it as a label and disregard it when performing calculations. The apostrophe will not be visible in the cell, but will be shown in the formula bar when the cell is selected.

Figure 2-6 Entering values into the worksheet

Excel 2000

Sales and expense values entered into the worksheet

Microsoft Excel - Profit1.xls											
	A	B	C	D	E	F	G	H	I	J	K	L
1												
2	Income and Expenditures for Kay's Hound Accessories											
3	File name: Profit1.xls											
4	Author: Kay Samoy			Date:4/6/00								
5	Ranges:			Macros:		Assumptions: Sales Growth						
6												
7		Quarter 1	Quarter 2	Quarter 3	Quarter 4							
8	Income											
9	Sales	970000	1000400	1210305	1484032							
10												
11	Expenses											
12	Rent	45000	45000	45000	45000							
13	Salaries	30000	30000	51750	61750							
14	Misc.	10200	8188	7900	9940							
15	Total Expenses											
16												
17												
18												
19												
20												
21												
22												

Sheet1 / Sheet2 / Sheet3

Ready   NUM

To practice entering values, follow the instructions on the **Prac2-2** tab of the practice file **MyPractice 2.xls**.

Hot Tip

If you wish to use the numeric keypad to enter numbers into a cell the Num Lock must be turned on.

 **Entering Formulas**

Concept

Formulas allow Excel to perform calculations such as averages, sums, or products using values that have been entered into the worksheet.

Do It!

Kay would like to calculate the total expenses and profits for each quarter.

1 Click cell B15 to activate it. This is the cell where the formula will be entered, and where the calculated result will appear.

2 Enter the following formula into the active cell: =B12+B13+B14. Notice that part of the label Total Expenses in cell A15 disappeared. You will learn how to widen columns in Lesson 3. The equals sign preceding the cell addresses and arithmetical operators prompts Excel to recognize the information as a formula. This calculation will result in a sum of the values in the three cells referenced in the formula.

3 Click the Enter button. The result, 85200, takes the place of the formula you entered in cell B15, and the formula remains visible in the formula bar, as shown in **Figure 2-7**.

4 Repeat steps 1-3 to enter similar formulas into cells C15, D15 and E15, substituting C, D, and E respectively for the Bs used above in the formula's cell addresses.

5 Click cell A17 to activate it and enter the label Profit into the cell. Profit is the result of Income, or Sales, minus Total Expenses.

6 Click cell B17 and enter the formula =B9-B15 into the cell, then press [Tab]. Excel subtracts First Quarter Expenses from First Quarter Sales to arrive at 884800, the profit for the First Quarter.

7 Repeat the previous step to enter similar formulas into cells C17, D17 and E17, substituting C, D, and E respectively for the Bs used above in the formula's cell addresses. Your worksheet should now resemble the one shown in **Figure 2-8**.

8 Save your workbook.

More

As you have seen, Excel formulas use cell addresses and the arithmetical operators; + for addition and – for subtraction. Since the standard computer keyboard does not contain multiplication or division symbols, the asterisk (*) is used for multiplication, and the forward slash (/) is used for division to specify the desired calculation. Using cell addresses, called cell referencing, helps Excel keep your calculations accurate by automatically recalculating results whenever the value in a cell referenced in a formula is altered.

Figure 2-7 Entering a formula

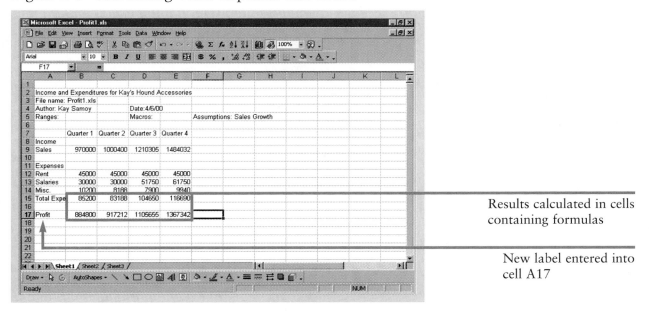

Formula displayed in
the formula bar

Results calculated using
the entered formula

Label in A15
partially covered

Figure 2-8 Calculating Total Expenses and Profit

Results calculated in cells
containing formulas

New label entered into
cell A17

Practice

To practice entering formulas, follow the
instructions on the **Prac2-3** tab of the practice file **MyPractice 2.xls**.

Hot Tip

If you select two or more cells that contain
values, their sum will appear in the status
bar. Right-clicking the sum in the status
bar will open a pop-up menu that allows you
to select other forms of tabulation.

Using Functions

Concept

Instead of having to create a new formula each time you wish to perform a simple calculation in a worksheet, you can use one of Excel's predefined formulas, called functions. Excel has hundreds of these built-in formulas, covering many of the most common types of calculations performed by spreadsheets.

Do It!

Kay wants to use the SUM function to calculate her Total Expenses.

1 Click cell B15 to make it active.

2 Press [Delete] to clear the previously entered formula. The data disappears allowing the contents of cell A15 to be visible.

3 Click the AutoSum button Σ. The AutoSum function automatically sets up the formula for adding together the values directly above the active cell. The sum formula (=SUM B12:B14) appears in cell B15 and in the formula bar. The cells being added, called the argument, are indicated with an animated border (**Figure 2-9**). The sum formula contains the notation B12:B14, called a range, which refers to all cells between B12 and B14.

4 Press [Enter] to confirm Excel's assumption and apply the formula to the worksheet. The value 85200 appears in the cell.

5 Click cell F7, then enter the label Total for Year.

6 Click cell F9 to make it the active cell.

7 Click the AutoSum button Σ. The SUM function appears in the cell followed by the correct range B9:E9. Since there are no values above the active cell, AutoSum uses the values in the cells to the left of the cell pointer.

8 Click the Enter button. The value 4664737 now appears in the cell, as shown in **Figure 2-10**.

9 Save your worksheet.

More

In the example above, you used the AutoSum button to enter the SUM function into Cell B15 in place of the formula =B9+C9+D9+E9. But, unlike AutoSum, most Excel functions require the user to manually enter additional information after the function name. This information, enclosed in parentheses and called the argument, can be cell references or other data which the function needs to produce a result. The function acts upon the argument, as the SUM function above acted on the range of cells enclosed in the parentheses that followed it.

Figure 2-9 Using the AutoSum function

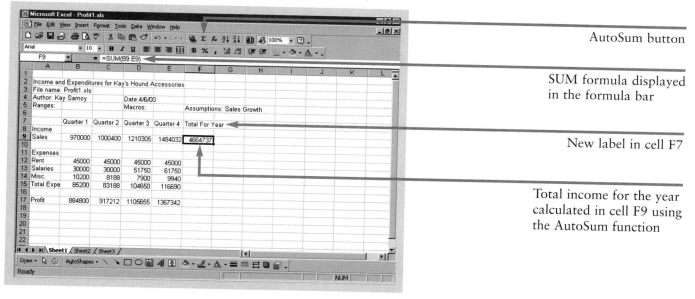

		Quarter 1	Quarter 2	Quarter 3	Quarter 4
6					
7		Quarter 1	Quarter 2	Quarter 3	Quarter 4
8	Income				
9	Sales	970000	1000400	1210305	1484032
10					
11	Expenses				
12	Rent	45000	45000	45000	45000
13	Salaries	30000	30000	51750	61750
14	Misc.	10200	8188	7900	9940
15	Total Expe	=SUM(B12:B14)		104650	116690
16					
17	Profit	970000	917212	1105655	1367342
18					

Animated border indicating the argument of the formula

SUM formula

Excel 2000

Figure 2-10 Calculating the total expenses for the year

AutoSum button

SUM formula displayed in the formula bar

New label in cell F7

Total income for the year calculated in cell F9 using the AutoSum function

Practice

To practice using functions, follow the instructions on the **Prac2-4** tab of the practice file **MyPractice 2.xls**.

Hot Tip

Any range of cells may be selected as the argument for an AutoSum. Click the cell in which you wish the result to appear, click the AutoSum button, then select a new argument for the function by clicking and dragging over the desired range.

Using the Paste Function Feature

Concept

To enter a function other than SUM, you can either enter it yourself or use the Paste Function command. The Paste Function command allows you to insert built-in formulas into your worksheet, saving you the trouble of remembering mathematical expressions and the time it takes to type them.

Do It!

Kay would like to use the Paste Function command to calculate the average total quarterly expenses for the year.

1. Click cell B19 to activate it.

2. Click Insert, then click Function. The Paste Function dialog box will open (see Figure 2-11), and an equals sign will appear in the selected cell indicating that a formula is to follow.

3. Click Average in the Function name box to select it. A description of what the Average function does will appear below the function category and name boxes.

4. Click OK. The Paste Function dialog box will disappear, and the Formula Palette will appear with the range B17:B18 listed as the argument in the Number1 text box. Since this is not the correct range of cells, a new range must be specified as the argument.

5. To select the range for the total expenses, click cell B15, then drag to cell E15. An animated border will appear around the selected cells, and as you drag, the Edit Formula dialog box will reduce itself to the Number1 text box displaying the selected range. When you release the mouse button, the Formula Palette will reappear in full and the formula =AVERAGE (B15:E15) will appear in the formula bar and in cell B19, as shown in Figure 2-12.

6. Click OK. The Formula Palette closes and cell B19 will display the result 97432.

7. Click cell A19, then label it Ave. Exp. Your worksheet should now resemble the one shown in Figure 2-13.

8. Save your worksheet.

More

When the Paste Function dialog box appears, the default setting for the function category is Most Recently Used. If you have not used the Paste Function command before, this category contains a default list of commonly used functions. Each function on this list can also be found under a more specific category. To find other functions, you can select other categories by clicking on them. The list of Function Names changes to correspond to the category you have chosen.

You may have noticed that the title of the upper text box on the Formula Palette, Number1, is in bold face whereas the title of the text box beneath it is not. The bold title indicates that data must be entered in the box in order for the function to work. Plain text indicates that entering text is optional.

Figure 2-11 Paste Function dialog box

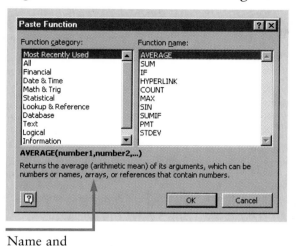

Name and description of the selected function

Figure 2-12 Selecting an argument for a function

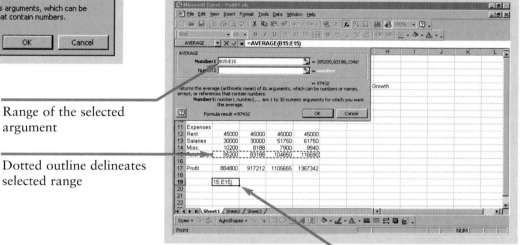

Range of the selected argument

Dotted outline delineates selected range

Formula is entered into the active cell with the selected range inserted as the argument

Figure 2-13 Pasted function

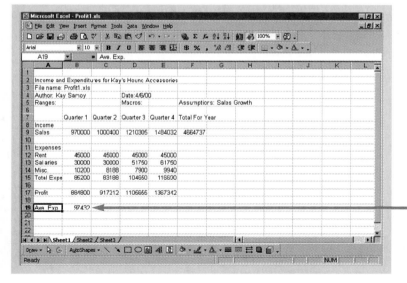

Result of the pasted function

Practice

To practice inserting functions, follow the instructions on the **Prac2-5** tab of the practice file **MyPractice 2.xls**.

Hot Tip

Instead of using the mouse to select an argument for a function in the Formula Palette, you can enter a range of cells using the keyboard.

Copying and Pasting Formulas

Concept

Formulas can be copied and pasted into other cells just like values or labels. Unless instructed otherwise, Excel considers the cell referred to in an argument to be a relative cell address. This means that if you copy a formula or function into another cell, Excel will substitute new cell references that are in the same position relative to the new formula or function location.

Do It!

To calculate the annual totals for her various expenses, Kay will copy the SUM function from cell F9 and paste it into cells F12, F13, F14, and F15.

1. Click cell F9 to activate it. The SUM function appears in the formula bar with the argument B9:E9.

2. Click the Copy button to copy the formula to the Windows Clipboard. An animated border appears around cell F9.

3. Click cell F12 to select it.

4. Click the Paste button to insert the copied function into the active cell. The result 180000 appears in cell F12. Notice that Excel has changed the argument in the formula bar from B9:F9 to B12:E12, the range of cell addresses relative to the copied function's position in the worksheet, so that the function will be applied to the row it is in rather than the one it was copied from.

5. Click the fill handle of the cell pointer surrounding cell F12 and drag down to cell F15. A gray border, shown in **Figure 2-14**, will appear around the range as you drag to indicate the target cells.

6. Release the mouse button. The SUM formula will be copied into cells F13, F14, and F15. Check your results against those in **Figure 2-15**.

7. Save the workbook as Profit1.xls.

More

Using relative cell references is similar to giving directions that explain where to go from the present location. Relative cell references follow the same directional instructions regardless of your starting position, such as "the four cells to the left of" or "the three cells above." In the preceding example, the formula told Excel to calculate the average of the values in the four cells to the left of the cell containing the formula. Wherever that formula is pasted, Excel will examine the four cells to the left of the target cell for values. Any cells that are blank, or do not contain values (such as those with labels), will be included in the calculation as zero. If you had attempted to paste the AVERAGE formula used above into a cell in column B, there would not be enough cells to the left of the target cell to fulfill the required argument, and the error message #REF! would have appeared in the cell.

Figure 2-14 Copying a formula using the fill handle

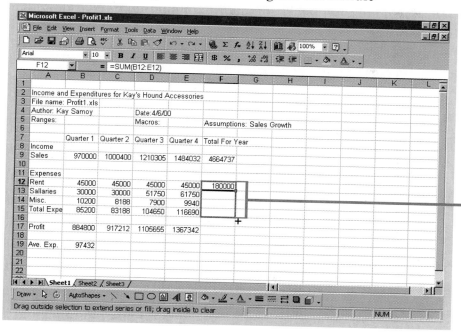

Formula will be pasted into these cells when the fill handle is released

Figure 2-15 Results of copied formula

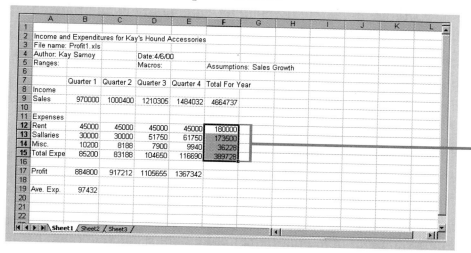

Pasted formulas calculated with appropriate cell references

Practice

To practice copying and pasting formulas, follow the instructions on the **Prac2-6** tab of the practice file **MyPractice 2.xls**.

Hot Tip

You can select which characteristics of a cell's data you wish to paste by using the **Paste Special** command on the Edit menu.

Using What-If Analysis

Concept

Excel makes it easy for you to change certain conditions in your worksheet, allowing you to see how these changes affect the results of various spreadsheet calculations. This is called What-If analysis, and is one of Excel's most useful features. It can be used to produce hypothetical and true projections of your data. Businesses benefit from this type of analysis because they can gain insight into the future with it and act accordingly.

Do It!

Kay wants to see what her sales would have been in Quarters 2, 3, and 4, assuming they grew 10% from the amount shown for the first quarter ($970,000).

1. Select the contents of cells C9, D9, and E9. These are the sales figures for the second, third, and fourth quarters and will be recalculated with the new assumption.

2. Press [Delete] to remove the values from the selected cells. Notice that the values in cells F9 and C15:E15 change. This is due to the fact that Excel automatically recalculates formulas when values in their referenced cells have been altered. The values in cells C9:E9 are now considered to be zero.

3. Click cell I5 to select it.

4. Enter .1 (10% expressed as a decimal) into the active cell. This is the cell that will be referenced in the formula that calculates projected earnings.

5. Click cell C9 to select it. Notice that Excel inserts a zero before the .1 in cell I5 as a place holder.

6. Now you must create a formula to multiply first quarter sales by 110%, which will show the results of a 10% increase. Enter the formula =B9*(1+$I$5) into the active cell, as shown in **Figure 2-16**. The dollar signs preceding the column letter I and the row number 5 tell Excel not to change the cell address, even if the formula is moved to a new location. This is known as an absolute cell reference.

7. Press [Enter]. The result of the calculation, 1067000, appears in place of the formula in cell C9. Cell F9 and B17 both change to reflect Excel's recalculation of their formulas, which include the cell C9 in their argument.

Figure 2-16 Using absolute cell references to perform What-If analysis

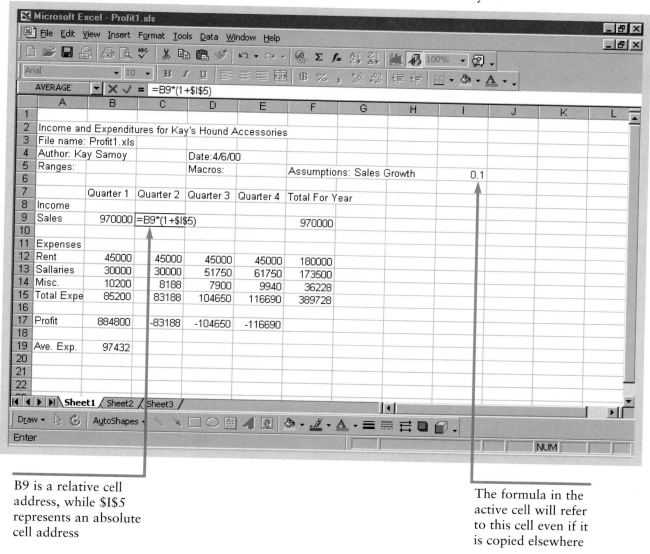

B9 is a relative cell address, while $I$5 represents an absolute cell address

The formula in the active cell will refer to this cell even if it is copied elsewhere

Excel 2000

Using What-If Analysis (continued)

Do It!

8 Click the Copy button ⬚ to copy the cell's formula to the Clipboard. A animated border appears around cell C9 to indicate that the selection is ready to be copied.

9 Click cell D9 to activate it, then click the Paste button ⬚. The pasted formula appears in the formula bar and the result, 1173700, appears in the cell. Notice that the reference to cell B9 has changed to C9, but that the reference to cell I5 remains the same. If the dollar signs had not been included, the copied formula would have replaced the cell reference I5 with J5, an empty cell, and the result would have been wrong.

10 Click cell E9 to activate it, then click the Paste button ⬚. As before, the formula is pasted and a new result, 1291070, appears in the cell, as shown in **Figure 2-17**.

11 Press [Enter] to confirm that the correct formula has been pasted into the target cell.

12 Click the Save button ⬚ to save your work.

More

Formulas can contain several operations. An operation is a single mathematical step in solving an equation, such as adding two numbers or calculating an exponent. When working with formulas that contain multiple operators, such as 12/200+4*8, Excel performs the calculations in the following order:

1. Parentheses
2. Exponents
3. Multiplication and division, from left to right
4. Addition and subtraction, from left to right

Operations inside parentheses are calculated first, in accordance with the rules above. For example, in the calculation 12/200+4*8, the operations would be performed as follows: first, 12 would be divided by 200, then four would be multiplied by 8, and finally the two results would be added together. If the equation was 12/(200+4)*8, then the operations would be calculated like this: first, 200 would be added to 4, then 12 would be divided by the result, and finally the dividend would be multiplied by 8.

Figure 2-17 Copying a formula containing an absolute cell address

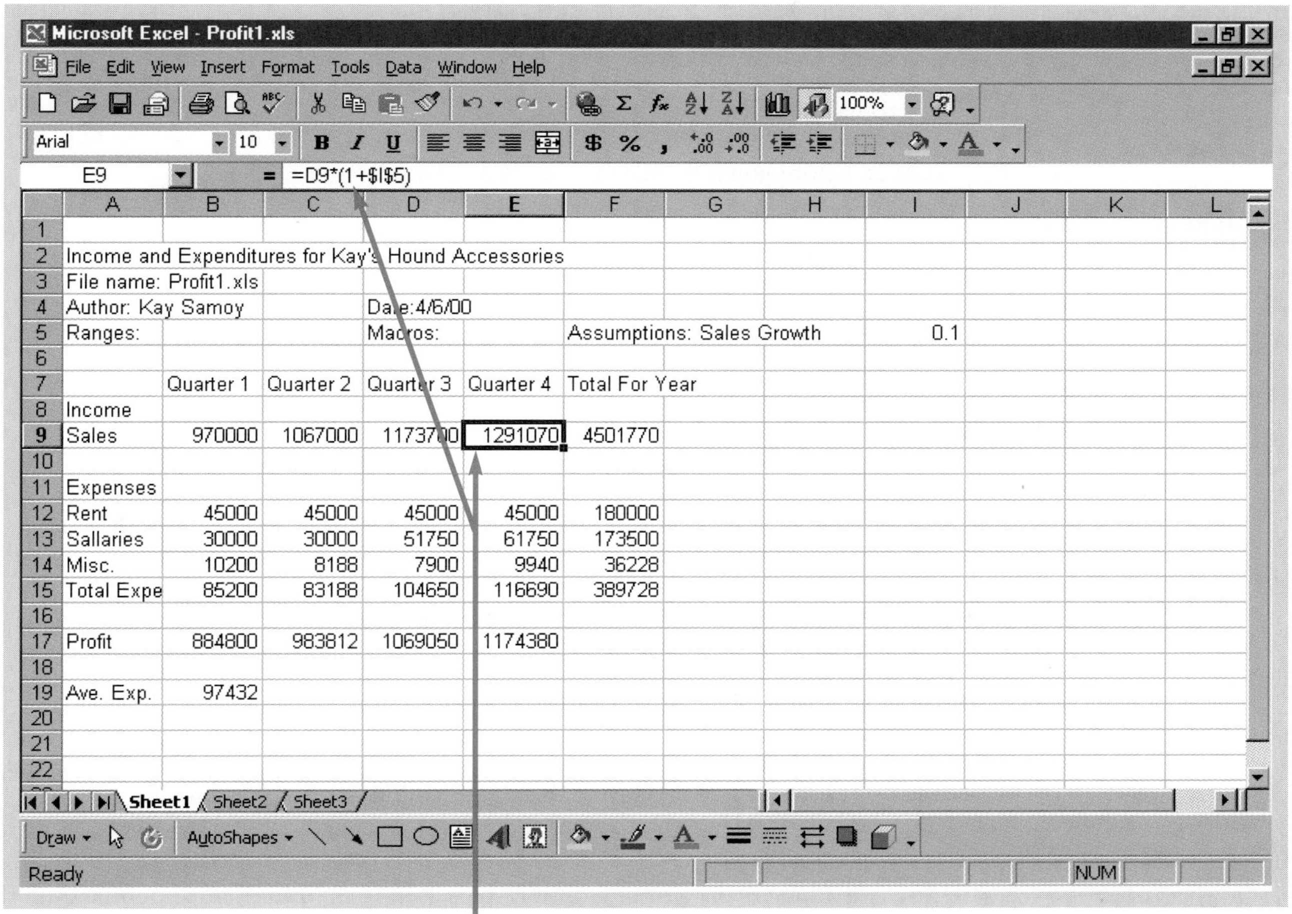

Though the relative cell address changed from B9 to D9 when the formula was copied, the absolute address for cell I5 remains unchanged

Practice

To practice using absolute cell references and What-If analysis, follow the instructions on the **Prac2-7** tab of the practice file **MyPractice 2.xls**.

Hot Tip

If you want both the column and row in a cell reference to remain absolute, then a $ must be placed in front of each. Placing a $ before only one part of the reference will make only that part absolute, while the other remains relative.

Previewing and Printing a Worksheet

Concept

Printing your worksheet is useful if you would like to have a paper copy to file, reference, or distribute to others. While offices are becoming more and more electronic, many people still prefer working with paper documents to viewing them on a screen. Excel allows you to view the worksheet as it will appear on the printed page before it is printed so that you can spot errors or items you would like to change before going through the printing process.

Do It!

Kay will display her worksheet in Print Preview mode, then print it.

1. Make sure your computer is properly connected to a working printer. (Ask your instructor.)

2. Click the Print Preview button on the Standard toolbar. The worksheet will be displayed in Print Preview mode, as shown in **Figure 2-18**. The mouse pointer appears as a magnifying glass.

3. Click at the top of the preview page. The worksheet will be magnified so that you may examine it more closely, and the pointer will change to an arrow. Since gridlines are nonprinting items, they do not appear in the preview.

4. Click Print... on the Print Preview toolbar. The view will revert to regular mode and the Print dialog box, **Figure 2-19**, will open.

5. Click OK. The Print dialog box will close, a box will appear notifying you of the print job's progress, and the document will be sent to the printer.

More

You can adjust many printing options by selecting the Page Setup command on the File menu. The Page Setup dialog box will open with four tabs; Page, Margins, Header/Footer, and Sheet. The Page tab controls the way in which the printed selection will appear on the page, such as its horizontal or vertical orientation, or by how much or little it is magnified. The Margins tab allows you to adjust the amount of space between printed matter and the edges of the page. The Header/Footer tab allows you to enter items that will appear at the top or bottom of each page, such as page numbers, titles, file names, or the name of the author. The Sheet tab lets you select how your data is presented on the printed page, such as whether or not you want to print gridlines, which parts of the worksheet you wish to print, and whether you want column headings to be repeated across each new page.

Figure 2-18 Previewing you worksheet

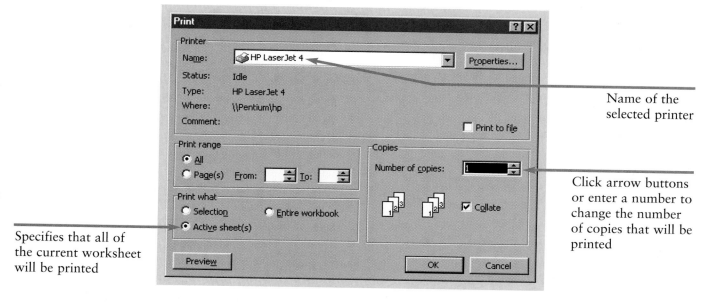

Click with magnifier
to zoom in

Figure 2-19 Print dialog box

Name of the
selected printer

Click arrow buttons
or enter a number to
change the number
of copies that will be
printed

Specifies that all of
the current worksheet
will be printed

Practice

To practice previewing and printing work-sheets, follow the instructions on the **Prac2-8** tab of the practice file **MyPractice 2.xls**.

Hot Tip

If you do not need to conduct a print preview or adjust the settings in the Print dialog box, you can print the active work-sheet by clicking the Print button on the Standard toolbar.

Shortcuts

Function	Button/Mouse	Menu	Keyboard
Copy data to the Clipboard		Click Edit, then click Copy	[Ctrl]+[C]
Cut data to the Clipboard		Click Edit, then click Cut	[Ctrl]+[X]
Paste data from the Clipboard		Click Edit, then click Paste	[Ctrl]+[V]
AutoSum	Σ		
Paste Function	*fx*	Click Insert, then click Function	
Print Preview		Click File, then click Print Preview	
Print	(to skip Print dialog box)	Click File, then click Print (for Print dialog box)	[Ctrl]+[P] (for Print dialog box)

Identify Key Features

Name the items indicated by callouts in **Figure 2-20**.

Figure 2-20 Features of an Excel screen and worksheet

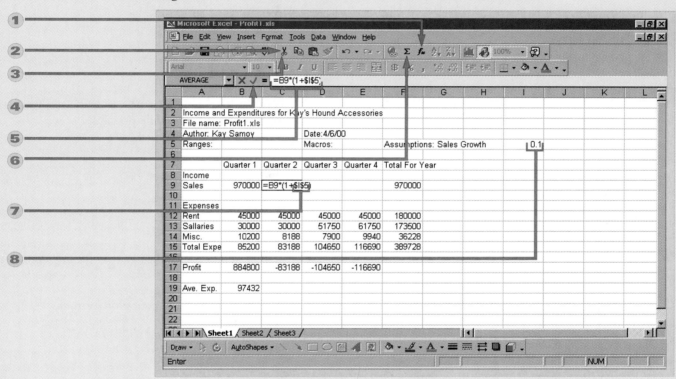

Excel 2000

Select The Best Answer

9. The small square in the lower-right corner of the active cell

10. A temporary storage space for cut or copied information

11. Use this symbol to represent multiplication in a formula

12. Allows you to view a worksheet as it will appear on an actual page

13. Lets you adjust margins or switch the page orientation

14. Offers AVERAGE as one of its choices

15. Aligned to the right by default

16. Type this symbol to designate a cell reference as absolute

a. Page Setup dialog box

b. Print Preview

c. Paste Function dialog box

d. Dollar sign

e. Fill handle

f. Clipboard

g. Asterisk

h. Values

Quiz (continued)

Complete the Statement

17. When using the fill handle, cells to be filled are indicated by a:

    a. ScreenTip

    b. Plus sign

    c. Check mark

    d. Gray border

18. Typing an apostrophe before a number instructs Excel to recognize it as a:

    a. Label

    b. Value

    c. Function

    d. Formula

19. All of the following actions will erase the Clipboard except:

    a. Pasting an item

    b. Cutting a new item

    c. Copying a new item

    d. Turning off the computer

20. By default, Excel considers referenced cell addresses to be:

    a. Absolute

    b. Copied from the Clipboard

    c. Relative

    d. AutoSums

21. Changing conditions to see how the results affect spreadsheet calculations is called:

    a. Absolute analysis

    b. Variable analysis

    c. Assumption analysis

    d. What-If analysis

22. To copy cell contents to a new location, drag-and-drop the cell pointer while pressing:

    a. [Shift]

    b. [Enter]

    c. [Tab]

    d. [Ctrl]

23. An animated border indicates that the cell contents:

    a. Will be deleted

    b. Are the result of a function or formula

    c. Have been sent to the Clipboard

    d. Have been pasted

24. The information enclosed in parentheses in a function is called the:

    a. Quantifier

    b. Argument

    c. Cell reference

    d. AutoSum

Interactivity

Test Your Skills

1. Enter values into your spreadsheet:

   a. Open the file you created in the first lesson, Test 1.xls.

   b. Fill in values to display how many hours you spend on each activity every day. For example, if you have four hours of class on Monday, enter the number 4 in the cell where the Monday column intersects with the Class row.

   c. If any of the values are repeated during the week, use the copy and paste commands to copy them from one cell to the others.

2. Use the AutoSum function to total the number of hours you spend on each activity during the week.

   a. Create a Total Hours label in the same row as the days of the week labels, in the column directly to the right of the Sunday column.

   b. Use AutoSum to enter the total hours you spend in Class in the cell where the Total Hours column and the Class row intersect.

   c. Use the fill handle to copy the AutoSum function into the next five cells in the Total Hours column in order to calculate the Total Hours for the remaining daily activities.

3. Calculate the average time you spend on each activity each week by using the Paste Function command:

   a. Enter the label Average in the cell directly to the right of Total Hours.

   b. Select the cell where the Average column intersects with the Class row. Then use the Paste Function command to place the average number of hours spent in class during the week in the active cell.

   c. Place the averages for the five other daily activities in the Average column by using the fill handle.

4. Preview and print the worksheet:

   a. Switch to Print Preview mode.

   b. Zoom in on the right side of the worksheet.

   c. Change the orientation of the page to Landscape.

   d. Print the worksheet.

   e. Return to normal view and save the file as Test 2.xls.

Interactivity (continued)

Problem Solving

1. Using the skills you have learned so far, create a spreadsheet that will allow you to track your individual monthly expenses for a year. Divide the year into four quarters, and use category labels such as rent, phone bill, books or supplies, food, entertainment, etc. Calculate your total expenses for each quarter, as well as your average quarterly expenses. Also include an assumption value of five percent to account for going over your allotted budget. Then conduct a What-If analysis to recalculate your total and average expenses based on a five percent increase in one of the categories. Save the file as Solved 2.xls.

2. Open the file Solved-HR.xls, which you created at the end of Lesson 1. To review, you designed this spreadsheet to detail how you will use the $10,000 dollar increase in your Human Resources expense account to improve recruiting. Now it is time to put the spreadsheet to work. Enter values to fill in the existing structure. Then add a label for a cell in which you can add up the different monetary allotments to demonstrate that you have not surpassed the $10,000 amount. Use a formula or function to calculate this total. Print a copy of the file, and then save the it as Solved-HR2.xls.

3. Open the file Solved-Rest.xls, which you also created in Lesson 1. Using fictional names and hours, complete the weekly waitstaff schedule that you designed. If your worksheet does not already have one, include a column that will store the total hours for each staff member each day, one for total hours for the week, and one for average hours per day. Using the skills you learned in this lesson, instruct Excel to calculate the data for these columns. When you have finished, print the worksheet and save it as Solved-Rest2.xls.

LESSON

3

FORMATTING WORKSHEET ELEMENTS

A s you work with your spreadsheet, you will find that you use certain groups of cells that contain related data repeatedly. Excel allows you to define these groups as ranges, and name them as you see fit. Then, rather then select the range by dragging the mouse over it, you can select the appropriate cells quickly and accurately with the name box.

Formatting refers to changing the appearance of information in a worksheet without changing its actual content. You can use Excel's many formatting tools to improve the appearance and the effectiveness of your spreadsheet. Text formatting includes font, font size, style, color, and alignment. Labels can also be formatted in a variety of styles, some of which help to express the kind of data they represent. You can format individual cells or ranges of cells. The AutoFormat command permits you to apply a set of predesigned formats to an entire range at once.

Although the structure of an Excel spreadsheet is highly organized, it is also very flexible. You can change the structure by increasing or decreasing column widths and row heights. You can also add and delete rows and columns as necessary. Changes to the structure of your worksheet depend on the data it contains and the formatting you have applied.

CASE STUDY
Kay will continue to develop and organize her spreadsheet by naming her ranges and adding formatting to her data. She will also modify the physical structure of the worksheet in order to improve its layout.

Defining and Naming Ranges

Concept

A range is any group of two or more cells, usually contiguous. The range B12 to E12 consists of these two cells, called anchor cells, and all cells between them. The data for this range is Kay's rent. Range addresses are defined by citing the first and last cell in the range separated by a colon. The address for the range for Kay's rent is B12:E12. Ranges are named so that they are easy to locate. These names can also be used in formulas. You can name a range using the Name Box or the Define Name dialog box.

Do It!

Kay wants to define and name all of the ranges in her worksheet that contain data.

1. Click cell B9, then drag to cell F9 to select these cells. The range for Sales is defined as B9:F9, and will be highlighted.

2. Click the inside the Name Box [B9 ▼]. The cell name B9 will become active, indicated by its highlighting.

3. Type Sales, then press [Enter]. The range B9:F9 is now named Sales, and the range name will appear in the Name Box whenever cells B9 to F9 are selected.

4. Repeat this process to name the remaining row labels, being sure to press [Enter] after each range name. Name the range B12:E12 Rent, the range B13:E13 Salaries, the range B14:E14 Miscellaneous, the range B15:E15 Total_Expenses, and the range B17:E17 Profit. Be sure to include the underscore ([Shift]+[-]) in the name Total_Expenses, as range names cannot contain any spaces. When you click the Name box drop-down arrow your Name Box list should now resemble the one shown in **Figure 3-1**.

Figure 3-1 Defining and naming ranges

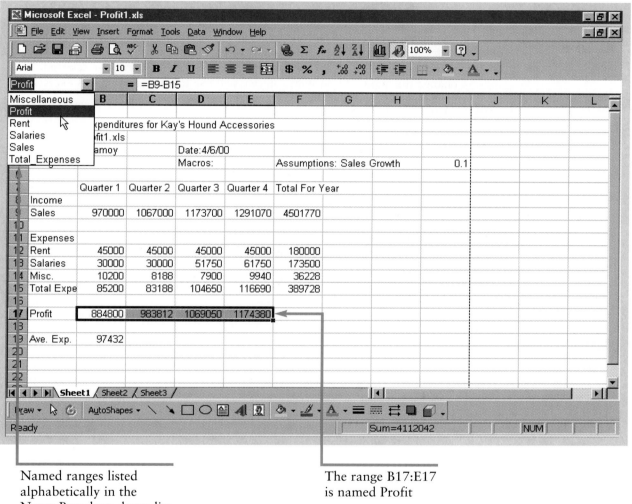

Named ranges listed
alphabetically in the
Name Box drop-down list

The range B17:E17
is named Profit

 # Defining and Naming Ranges (continued)

Do It!

5 Click cell B8, and drag down to cell B17. The range B8:B17 will be selected.

6 Click Insert, highlight Name, then click Define. The Define Name dialog box, shown in **Figure 3-2**, will open with the range name Quarter_1 in the Names in Workbook text box. Excel automatically picks up a column or row label as the default range name if it is adjacent to, or included in, the range selected. You can change this name if you wish, but we will use the defaults for this exercise.

7 Click [OK] to name the range.

8 Click cell C8, then hold [Shift] down and click cell C17. The range C8:C17 will become highlighted. Holding the shift key down highlights all of the cells between the first and the last cells you select.

9 Repeat step six to name this range Quarter_2.

10 Use the Define Name dialog box to name the range D8:D17 Quarter_3, the range E8:E17 Quarter_4, and the range F8:F17 Total_for_Year.

11 Click elsewhere in the worksheet to deselect the range.

12 Click the Save button 🖫 to save the changes you have made to the worksheet.

More

Ranges do not have to be made up of cells that are touching. They can contain nonadjacent blocks of cells, or multiple nonadjoining cells. To create a nonadjacent range, highlight the first group of cells or a single cell that you wish to include, then hold down [Ctrl] while selecting the next cluster of cells. You can select as many noncontiguous cells or ranges as you desire. Clicking anywhere else in the worksheet will deselect the ranges.

Figure 3-2 Define Name dialog box

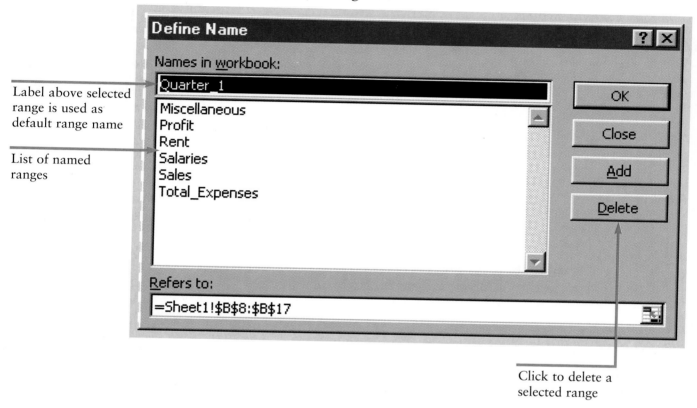

Label above selected range is used as default range name

List of named ranges

Click to delete a selected range

Excel 2000

 # Formatting Cell Contents

Concept

Formatting enhances the appearance of your worksheet and can make your labels stand out, so they will be easier to read. Formatting options include changing the font (typeface and size), style, and alignment of your text. A cell or range must be selected before formatting can be applied to it.

Do It!

Kay wants to add formatting to various cells to emphasize their contribution to the worksheet.

1. Click the Name box drop down arrow, then click Profit on the list of named ranges that appears. If Profit had not been visible, you would have had to use the scroll bar on the right edge of the list to access the rest of the range names it contains.

2. Click Format, then click Cells. The Format Cells dialog box will open.

3. Click the Font tab to bring it to the front of the stack, as shown in **Figure 3-3**.

4. Notice that the current font (Arial), font style (regular), and size (10 point) are highlighted. From the Font Style list, select Bold. The letters in the Preview box will be made bold so that you may view the results of this change before you apply it.

5. Click OK . The dialog box will close and the numbers contained in the range named Profit will appear bold, as shown in **Figure 3-4**.

6. Click cell A2 to make it active.

7. Click the Font box drop-down arrow. A list of the fonts installed on your computer will appear.

8. Drag the scroll bar box on the Font list down until Times New Roman is visible, then move the pointer over Times New Roman and click. The typeface of "Income and Expenditures for Kay's Hound Accessories" will change from Arial to Times New Roman.

9. Click the Font Size text box. The current point size of 10 will become highlighted, ready to be changed.

10. Type 14, then press [Enter]. The title will increase in size.

11. Select the range A2:K2. These are the columns across which the title will be centered.

12. Click the Merge and Center button 🔳 , then click elsewhere on the worksheet to deselect the columns. **Figure 3-5** shows the new title placement.

Figure 3-3 Format Cells dialog box

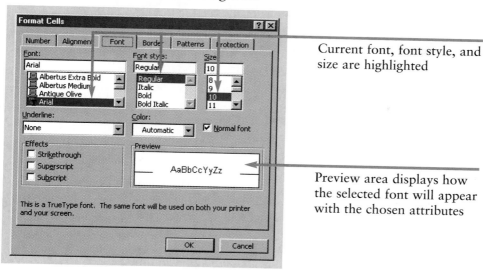

Current font, font style, and size are highlighted

Preview area displays how the selected font will appear with the chosen attributes

Figure 3-4 Bolding cell data

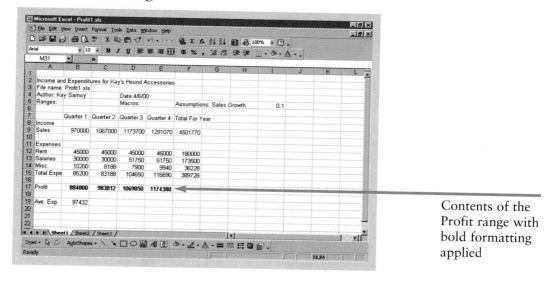

Contents of the Profit range with bold formatting applied

Figure 3-6 Formatted worksheet title

Font Size text box

Font box drop-down arrow

Worksheet title in 14 point, Times New Roman and centered across cells A through K

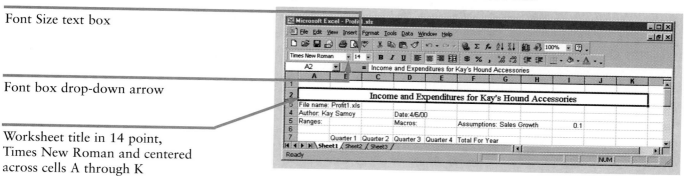

Excel 2000

Formatting Cell
Contents (continued)

Do It!

13 Select the range B7:F7.

14 Click the Italic button $\boxed{I}$. The column labels will change to italicized type.

15 Click the Underline button $\boxed{U}$. Each column label will be underlined. Notice that the Italic and Underline buttons are indented. An indented button indicates that a particular formatting option is being applied.

16 Select the range A8:A19.

17 Click the right edge, the arrow, of the Font Color button $\boxed{A}$. The Font Color palette, shown in **Figure 3-6**, will open.

18 Select the blue color box in the second row of the palette, then click anywhere on the worksheet to deselect the range. The row labels will change to blue. Your worksheet should appear as the one shown in **Figure 3-7**.

19 Click File, then click Save to save your work.

More

The Font tab in the Format Cells dialog box allows you to change most of the attributes relating to text. The options Font, Font style, and Size each have two boxes attached to them. The lower box is a list box that indexes available fonts, font styles, and font sizes respectively. The upper box is a text box wherein you can enter any of these choices without having to scroll through the list. However, the point size of your font selection is not limited to only those numbers listed, and can be anywhere between 1 and 409.

The Underline option contains a drop-down list with five styles of underlines that can be used. The Color option contains a drop-down palette with 56 color choices. Clicking one of these boxes will turn your text that color. Checking the Normal Font box reverts any changed font formats to the default settings described above. There are three effects you can select: Strikethrough draws a line through text, making it appear as if it has been crossed out; Superscript shrinks the text and raises it above the baseline; Subscript shrinks and drops the text below the baseline. Any alteration to a font formatting characteristic that you make will appear in the preview window in the tab, and none of the changes made will take effect on the worksheet until the OK button is clicked.

Figure 3-6 Font Color palette

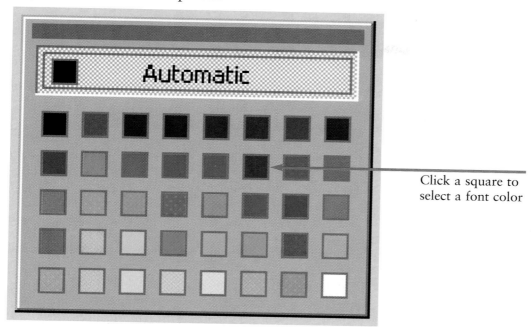

Click a square to
select a font color

Figure 3-7 Formatted cell contents

Italicized and underlined
cell labels

Cell labels with
color applied

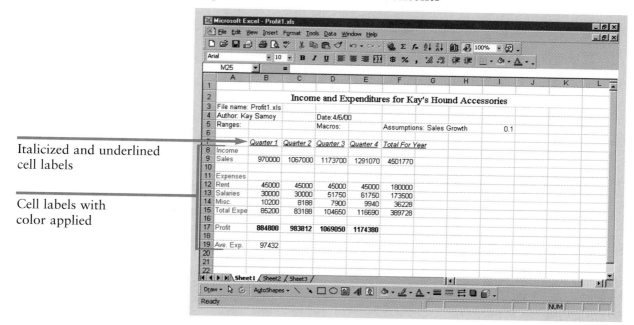

Practice

To practice formatting cell labels, follow the
instructions on the **Prac3-2** tab of the practice file **MyPractice3.xls**.

Hot Tip

Clicking an indented formatting button
removes the applied format and reverts the
button to its normal, flat, state.

Working with Rows and Columns

Concept

There are times when the information you enter into your worksheet will not fit neatly into a cell set with the default height and width. Therefore you may need to adjust the height of a row or, more commonly, the width of a column. The standard column width is 8.43 characters, but can be set anywhere between 0 and 255.

Do It!

Kay wants to widen some of the columns in her worksheet to accommodate long labels and values.

1. Move the mouse pointer onto the dividing line between the column A and column B heading buttons. The pointer will change from a cross ✛ to a double-arrow ✛ that will allow you to resize the column.

2. Click and hold the left mouse button. The gridline that divides the columns will become dotted and the column width will appear in a ScreenTip.

3. With the mouse button depressed, drag the column boundary to the right until the width reaches 13.00 characters. The entire label "Total Expenses" will be visible. While the "Total Expenses" label was cropped before you resized the column, notice that the label in cell F7, Total for Year, is fully visible. Excel will display a label that is longer than its cell is wide in its entirety as long as the cell it intrudes upon is empty.

4. Click the column B heading button to select the entire column.

5. While holding [Ctrl], click the column C, D, E, and F heading buttons so that all five columns are selected, as shown in **Figure 3-8**.

6. Click Format, highlight Column, then select Width from the submenu. The Column Width dialog box, **Figure 3-9**, will open.

7. Type 14 in the Column Width text box, then click ⬚ OK ⬚. Columns B through F will increase in width to 14 characters. This width is to accommodate formatting that you will apply to the cell data in a later skill.

8. Save your work.

More

You can also adjust the height of the rows in your worksheet. Row height is measured in points, just as fonts are, and there are 72 points per inch. Dragging the line between two row heading buttons is one way to change a row's height. There is a Row command on the Format menu that allows you to alter height as well. Row height usually does not need to be changed manually, as Excel will adjust row height to fit the largest point size of a cell's label or data.

Table 3-1 Column formatting commands

COMMAND	FUNCTION
Width	Adjust the width to a specified number of characters
AutoFit Selection	Adjust the width to fit the widest cell entry
Hide	Hides a selected column from view
Unhide	Displays a hidden column
Standard Width	Allows you to set a default width size, and resets selected columns to the specified size

Excel 2000

Figure 3-8 Selecting columns to be resized

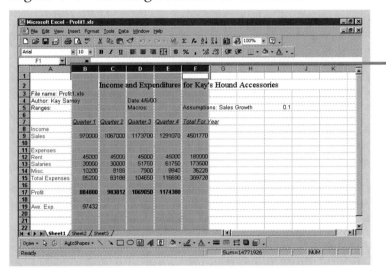

Columns B through F selected

Figure 3-9 Column Width dialog box

Practice

To practice working with column and row widths, follow the instructions on the **Prac3-3** tab of the practice file **MyPractice3.xls**.

Hot Tip

You can resize a column's width to fit the widest entry automatically by double-clicking the right edge of the column heading button.

Inserting and Deleting Rows and Columns

Concept

In Excel you can add and delete columns or rows to customize your worksheet to your specific needs. For example, you may want to add another column for new inventory products, or perhaps even delete a row that contains expenses that are no longer current.

Do It!

Kay wants to add an additional row between her documentation sections and the main body of her worksheet, and she wants to remove the column between Assumptions and the assumption value.

1 Click cell A6 to make it active.

2 Click Insert, then click the Cells command. The Insert dialog box, **Figure 3-10**, will open with the Shift cells down radio button selected.

3 Click the Entire Row radio button. This tells Excel to add a row and shift all of the rows below row 6 down.

4 Click [OK]. A new row will be inserted, the contents of the worksheet will shift down by one row, and your formulas will be updated to reflect the row shift.

5 Click cell H5 to make it active.

6 Click Edit, the click Delete. The Delete dialog box, similar to Insert, will open with the Shift Cells Left radio button selected.

7 Click the Entire column radio button, then click [OK]. Cell H5 will be deleted and the Sales Growth data will move from I5 to H5. Even though the Sales values for Quarters 2 through 4 are based on the absolute address of the assumption, Excel will recalculate the formulas based on the new cell address. Compare your worksheet with that of **Figure 3-11**.

8 Save your workbook.

More

A dummy column or dummy row is a blank column or row included at the end of a defined range that is used to hold a place or create blank space. A dummy row between a range of values and a cell containing a formula to average them allows Excel to include the added row in the range rather than considering it to be an unrelated value. Then, if a row or column is added to the original range, Excel will recalculate any formulas that include that range to include the change. If you need to add a row or column to a range that does not include a dummy, you must manually adjust your formulas to take into account the new cells and values. If a row or column is inserted into the middle of an existing range, Excel is able to recalculate any formulas that reference that range. It is only when you need to add a row or column to the end of an existing range that is being used in a formula that a dummy row or column becomes necessary.

Figure 3-10 Insert dialog box

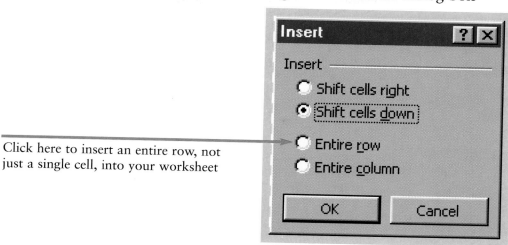

Click here to insert an entire row, not just a single cell, into your worksheet

Excel 2000

Figure 3-11 Worksheet with a row inserted and a cell deleted

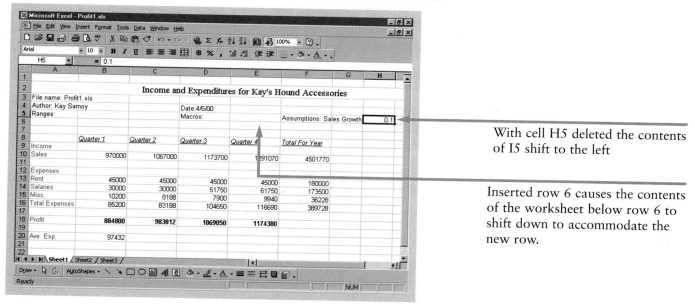

With cell H5 deleted the contents of I5 shift to the left

Inserted row 6 causes the contents of the worksheet below row 6 to shift down to accommodate the new row.

Practice

To practice inserting and deleting rows and columns, follow the instructions on the **Prac3-4** tab of the practice file **MyPractice3.xls**.

Hot Tip

Right-clicking (clicking the right mouse button) brings up various pop-up menus. Where you right-click in the Excel window will determine which pop-up menu appears. Try right-clicking various elements of the Excel window to view these menus.

Formatting Cell Values

Concept

Although labels can help identify what kind of data a number represents, you may want to format the values themselves so that their function is more apparent. Common formats include Currency, Percentage, Fraction, and Comma. The format you choose will depend on how the values are to be used, and how you wish them to appear. Cell or range formatting can be applied before or after data is entered.

Do It!

Kay wants to format all of her values with commas so that they will be easier to read, format the Profit range in Currency Style, format her assumption in Percentage Style, and then decrease the number of decimal places in cell B20.

1. Select the range B10:F20.

2. Click the Comma Style button 〖,〗. All of the cells contained within the selected range will be formatted in the Comma Style, which includes two decimal places.

3. Click the Name Box drop down list arrow, then click Profit on the list of ranges that appears. The range B18:F18 will be highlighted.

4. Click the Currency Style button 〖$〗. The values entered in the Profit row will appear with dollar signs preceding them and two decimal places to represent cents.

5. Click cell H5 to make it the active cell.

6. Click the Percentage Style button 〖%〗. The originally entered value of 0.1 will appear as 10%. The result of the formula whose argument references this cell will remain the same.

7. Click cell B20 to activate it.

8. Click the Decrease Decimal button 〖.00→.0〗 twice. The two decimal places will be erased. **Figure 3-12** displays the worksheet as it should now appear.

9. Save the worksheet.

More

When you applied the Currency, Comma, and Percentage Styles to the worksheet, you used the default settings for each of these buttons. The Number tab of the Format Cells dialog box, shown in **Figure 3-13**, can be accessed by selecting the Cells command on the Format menu. It allows you to apply one of twelve different formatting styles to cells. Most of the categories of formatting listed on the Numbers tab can be customized to suit the specific needs of your worksheet and personal preferences.

The number of decimal place values taken and the appearance of date and time references can be altered, special formats can be defined for use in databases, and custom number formats can be created for advanced users of Excel.

Figure 3-12 Cell values with formatting applied

Percentage Style

Comma Style

Currency Style

Decimal places
reduced by two

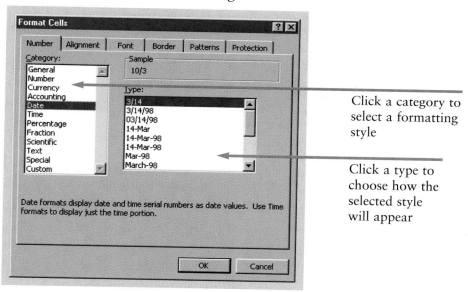

Figure 3-13 Format Cells dialog box

Click a category to
select a formatting
style

Click a type to
choose how the
selected style
will appear

Practice

To practice formatting cell values, follow the instructions on the **Prac3-5** tab of the practice file **MyPractice3.xls**.

Hot Tip

If a cell is too narrow to display a value correctly, Excel will display number signs (#####) in place of the data, though the actual value is unaffected. Making the cell wide enough to accommodate the data properly will make it reappear correctly.

Excel 2000

Using AutoFormat

Concept

The AutoFormat command allows you to add one of sixteen sets of formatting to selected ranges, creating tables that are easy to read and are visually stimulating. Numbers, borders, fonts, patterns, alignment, and the height and width of rows and columns can all be altered using the AutoFormat options. AutoFormat alters the appearance of tables using colors, fonts, and textures.

Do It!

Kay wants to use the AutoFormat function to improve the appearance of her worksheet and set the main body data off from the documentation.

1. Select the range A8:F20 to make this area active.

2. Click Format, then select the AutoFormat command. The AutoFormat dialog box, shown in **Figure 3-14** will open.

3. Drag the Table Format list box scroll bar down to reveal the lower portion of the Table Format list, then select 3D Effects 2.

4. Click ⬚ OK ⬚, then click anywhere in the worksheet to deselect the area. The range A8:F20 will appear as shown in **Figure 3-15**.

5. Select the range A3:H5 to make this group of cells active.

6. Click Format, then select AutoFormat to open the AutoFormat dialog box.

7. Select List 1 from the Table Format list, then click the Options button ⬚ Options >> ⬚. The AutoFormat dialog box will grow to display six format types which you can include or exclude when the AutoFormat is applied.

8. Click Font, Width/Height, and Alignment so they do not display a check in their check boxes. The Sample table will show how the range will look with these options off. These options were turned off so as to preserve the font, size and placement of the title and the width of the columns.

9. Click ⬚ OK ⬚, then click anywhere in the worksheet to deselect the range. **Figure 3-16** shows the worksheet documentation with the AutoFormatting.

10. Save your workbook.

Figure 3-14 AutoFormat dialog box

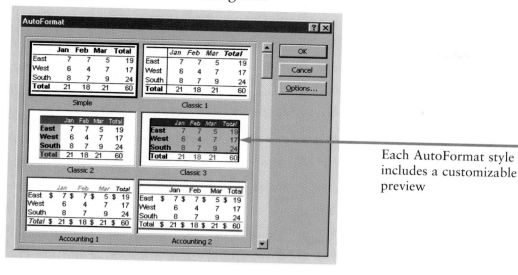

Each AutoFormat style includes a customizable preview

Figure 3-15 AutoFormatting applied to the selected range

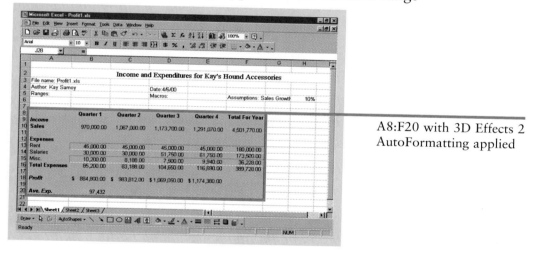

A8:F20 with 3D Effects 2 AutoFormatting applied

Figure 3-16 List 1 AutoFormatting applied

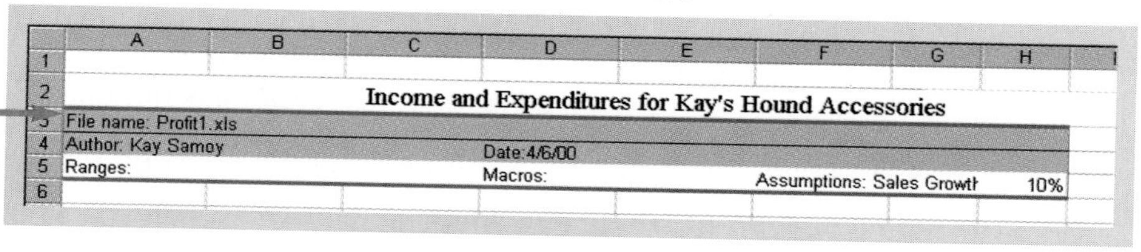

A3:H5 with List 1 AutoFormatting applied with Font, Width/Height, and Alignment left intact

Practice

To practice using AutoFormat, follow the instructions on the **Prac3-6** tab of the practice file **MyPractice3.xls**.

Hot Tip

The None option on the Table Format list in the AutoFormat dialog box will return a range to its original, unformatted style.

Excel 2000

Filling a Range with Labels

Concept

Excel can automatically fill a range with several types of series information. Series information includes numbers, numbers combined with text (such as Quarter 1), dates, and times. Excel can step, or increase, a series by a constant set value, or multiply by a constant factor. For example, you can add all the months of the year to a worksheet by typing only January and then extending the series. The way a series fills will depend on the type of value and the incremental setting.

Do It!

To practice the AutoFill feature, Kay will erase the Quarter column headings and then replace them with a series fill.

1 Click cell B8 to select it, then press the [Back Space] key to delete the cell label.

2 Repeat this process for cells C8, D8, and E8. The range B8:E8 will be empty.

3 Click cell B8, then type Quarter 1.

4 Move the mouse pointer to the fill handle of the cell pointer surrounding cell B8. It will change to the crosshairs.

5 Drag the pointer to cell E8 with the fill handle. As you drag the pointer, a dimmed border will appear indicating the cells that have been selected, and ScreenTips will appear showing what will be placed the cell where the mouse pointer currently is, as shown in **Figure 3-17**.

6 Release the mouse button. The range B8:E8 will be filled with Quarter 1 through Quarter 4.

7 Close your workbook without saving changes,

More

In the above example, you used **AutoFill** to enter a series of labels into a range of cells. Along with AutoFill, there are three other series fill types that you can use: Linear, Growth, and Date. These are advanced options and are found in the Series dialog box, shown in **Figure 3-18**, which can be accessed by clicking the Edit menu, selecting Fill, and then clicking Series on the submenu.

A Linear series fill, with the Trend box unchecked, adds the Step value to the value in the cell selected. With Trend checked, the Step value is disregarded and the trend is calculated based on the average of the difference between the values in the selected cells. This average is then used to fill the range by increasing or decreasing the value by a constant amount. If necessary, the original selected cell information is replaced to fit the trend.

A Growth series fill is similar to a Linear series fill, except that instead of adding values together, numbers are multiplied to create a geometric growth trend. A series created based upon dates uses the options in the Date Units list. You can extend selected dates by day, weekday, month, or year. The Stop value can be set so as to fix a value at which the series will end. If the selected range is filled before it reaches the Stop value, it will end at that point.

Figure 3-17 Filling a range with labels

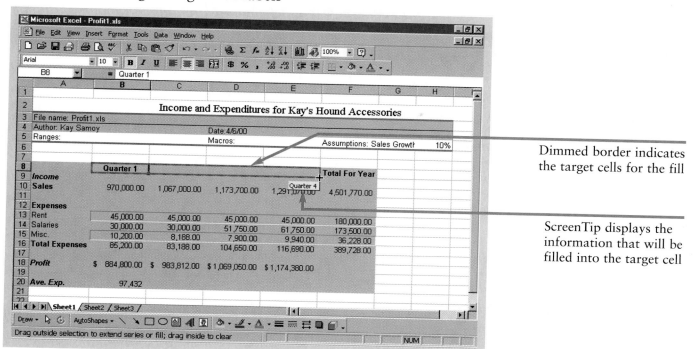

Dimmed border indicates the target cells for the fill

ScreenTip displays the information that will be filled into the target cell

Excel 2000

Figure 3-18 Series dialog box

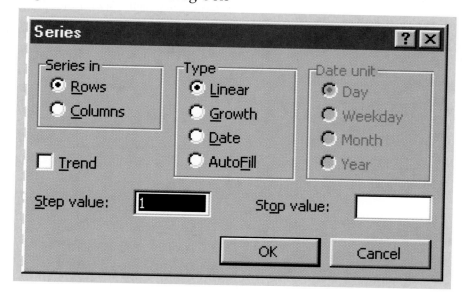

Practice

To practice filing ranges with labels follow the instructions on the **Prac3-7** tab of the practice file **MyPractice3.xls**.

Hot Tip

If you select a value, and then hold the right mouse button while dragging the fill handle, a pop-up menu will appear allowing you to choose the type of series that is inserted into the destination cells.

Formatting Cells and Ranges

Concept

As you have seen, you can format the contents of spreadsheet cells in order to make the spreadsheet more pleasing to the eye and more comprehensible. The AutoFormat command allows you to apply a set of formatting characteristics to the contents of cells or to a cell or range itself. Sometimes, however, you may want to exert more precise control over the appearance of a cell or range than AutoFormat permits. Excel gives you the ability to fill cells and ranges with colors and patterns, and outline them with special borders.

Do It!

Kay wants to experiment with adding a color pattern and a border to the title of her worksheet. She will then undo her experiment.

1. Click cell A2 to select the merged cell that contains the worksheet's title.

2. Click the arrow on the right edge of the Fill Color button. A color palette will open below the button.

3. Click the Rose color square in the bottom-left corner of the palette. The palette will close and the merged title cell will be filled with Rose.

4. Click Format, then click Cells. The Format Cells dialog box will open.

5. Click the Border tab to bring it to the front of the dialog box. In the Presets section of the tab, click the Outline button. In the Line Style section, select the dashed line (fourth down in the second column).

6. Click the Color selection arrow and choose the Dark Red square from the palette that appears. The Border tab should now look like **Figure 3-19**.

7. Click the Patterns tab to bring it to the front. Notice that the Rose color square is selected and shown in the Sample box because it has already been applied to the active cell.

8. Click the Pattern selection arrow. A color palette that includes patterns at the top will open. Click the Diagonal Stripe pattern (fourth from the left in the second row). The Pattern tab should now look like **Figure 3-20**.

9. Click OK to apply the border and pattern to the selected cell, and then deselect the cell, which should resemble **Figure 3-21**.

10. Click the arrow on the right edge of the Undo button and highlight the three Format Cells operations you just performed. Click the mouse to undo the actions.

More

The Font Color, Fill Color, and Borders buttons are all "loaded" with the last option (color or border type) you applied, which is displayed as part of the button's icon. To apply this option again, you do not need to click the button's arrow to open its palette. Simply click on the button itself.

Figure 3-19 Border tab

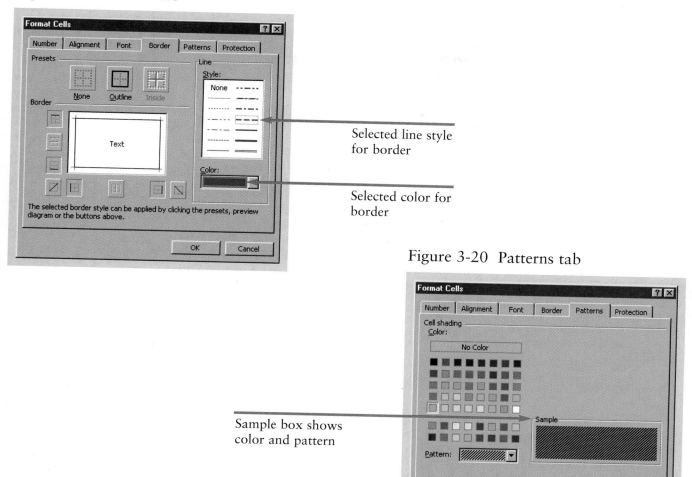

Figure 3-20 Patterns tab

Figure 3-21 Cell formatted with color, pattern, and border

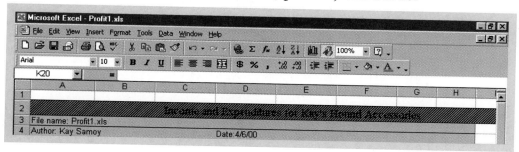

Practice

Open a new workbook. Then fill the range A1:D5 with the color Aqua, add an inside, dotted border to the range, and fill cell B2 with a yellow vertical stripe pattern. Do not save this exercise.

Hot Tip

Color and patterns should be used carefully as overuse and misuse can damage the effectiveness of your spreadsheet, as you may have discovered while completing this Skill.

Shortcuts

Function	Button/Mouse	Menu	Keyboard
Merge cells and center contents	⊞		
Merge cells		Click Format, then click Cells, then click Alignment	[Ctrl]+[1]
Make a label bold	**B**	Click Format, then click Cells, then click Font	[Ctrl]+[B]
Italicize a label	*I*	Click Format, then click Cells, then click Font	[Ctrl]+[I]
Underline a label	U	Click Format, then click Cells, then click Font	[Ctrl]+[U]
Add color to a label	A ▾	Click Format, then click Cells, then click Font	[Ctrl]+[1]
Comma Style	,	Click Format, then click Style	
Currency Style	$	Click Format, then click Style	
Percent Style	%	Click Format, then click Style	
Increase or Decrease decimal places	.00→ or ←.00		

Identify Key Features

Name the items indicated by callouts in **Figure 3-22**.

Figure 3-22 Formatting features

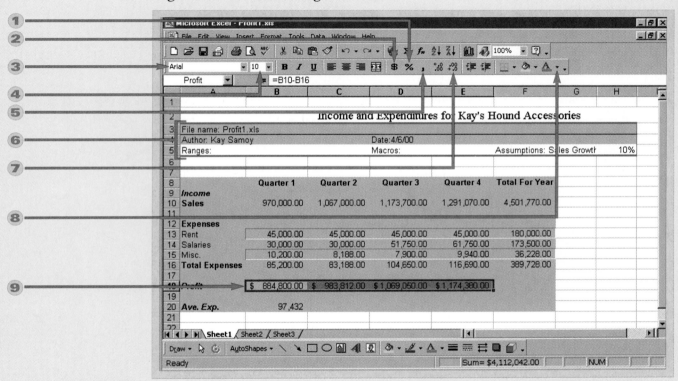

Select The Best Answer

10. Allows you to select a named range quickly and accurately

11. Contains a tab with options for changing font, font style, and font size

12. Combines the contents of multiple cells into one cell

13. Lets you add a set of predetermined formatting options to a spreadsheet

14. Contains the Bold, Italic, and Underline buttons

15. A group of two or more cells

16. Indicates that a particular formatting style is applied to the current selection

17. A blank column at the end of a defined range

a. Indented button

b. Formatting toolbar

c. Dummy column

d. Format Cells dialog box

e. AutoFormat command

f. Name box

g. Range

h. Merge and Center button

Quiz (continued)

Complete the Statement

18. All of the following are effects available on the Font tab of the Format Cells dialog box except:

    a. Strikethrough

    b. Strikescript

    c. Superscript

    d. Subscript

19. An appropriate way to express a range address is:

    a. B9/E9

    b. B9;E9

    c. B9-E9

    d. B9:E9

20. A range name may not contain:

    a. Uppercase letters

    b. Labels used in the spreadsheet

    c. Spaces

    d. Numbers

21. The Formatting toolbar offers all of the following formatting styles except:

    a. Currency Style

    b. Percentage Style

    c. Fraction Style

    d. Comma Style

22. The standard width of a worksheet column is:

    a. 8.43 characters

    b. 13.00 characters

    c. 13.5 characters

    d. 255 characters

23. All of the following can be done from the Insert menu except:

    a. Insert a blank row

    b. Insert a blank column

    c. Define and name a range

    d. Apply an AutoFormat

24. A 72 point character would be equal to:

    a. 1 inch

    b. 1 foot

    c. 8.43 centimeters

    d. 8.43 inches

25. 3D Effects 2 is a type of:

    a. Cell value

    b. Range name

    c. AutoFormat

    d. Function

26. All of the following are examples of series data you can enter in a worksheet except:

    a. Linear

    b. Growth

    c. Currency

    d. AutoFill

27. The largest font size in points is:

    a. 409

    b. 256

    c. 72

    d. 8.43

Interactivity

Test Your Skills

1. Define and name the ranges in a spreadsheet:

   a. Open the file Test 2.xls that you created at the end of the previous lesson.

   b. Define and name the following ranges using the name box: Class, Activities, Meals, Studying/Homework, Leisure, and Sleep.

   c. Define and name the following ranges by opening the Define name dialog box from the Insert menu: Monday, Tuesday, Wednesday, Thursday, Friday, Saturday, Sunday, Total Hours, and Average.

2. Format cell labels in a spreadsheet:

   a. Change the font of the title of your worksheet to Times New Roman, and then change its size to 12 point.

   b. Merge and center the title across the first ten columns of the worksheet.

   c. Add bold formatting to the days of the week labels. Italicize and underline the Total Hours and Average labels.

   d. Change the font color of the daily activities labels in Column A to red, and then make them bold.

3. Adjust the columns and rows in your spreadsheet:

   a. Click and drag the right border of Column A until the column is 18.00 characters wide.

   b. Click and drag the right border of the Wednesday column until the entire label "Wednesday" is visible.

   c. Double-click with the mouse to automatically resize the Total Hours column so that its label fits.

   d. Add an extra row between the documentation and data sections of your worksheet.

4. Add advanced formatting to your spreadsheet:

   a. Reduce all values in the Average column to three decimal places.

   b. Apply Comma Style to all values in the Total Hours column.

   c. Apply the AutoFormat 3D Effects 1 to the documentation section of the worksheet.

   d. Apply the AutoFormat Classic 3 to the data section of your worksheet, but preserve the font and width/height that the worksheet already has.

   e. Add an outside, solid blue border to the merged title cell.

   f. Fill the title cell with the color orange and the pattern Thin Horizontal Stripe.

   g. Save the file as Test 3.xls.

Interactivity (continued)

Problem Solving

1. Utilize the knowledge and skills you have acquired about spreadsheet design to keep yourself on track as you work toward earning a diploma. Using Excel, create a worksheet that displays your graduation requirements and the means by which you are fulfilling them. Include courses you may have already taken, your current courses, and the courses you will need and want to take in the future. Also include data such as the total number of credits you need to graduate and the percentage you have so far. Calculate how many credits you will need to average each academic semester. Then see if your actual numbers are on pace. Finally, be sure to take advantage of Excel's formatting features to enhance the organization and appearance of your spreadsheet. Save the file as Solved 3-Grad.xls.

2. Open Solved-HR2.xls, a file you saved at the end of the previous lesson. Define and name all relevant ranges in the worksheet. Format the entire worksheet in a professional manner, using both independent formatting techniques and one instance of the AutoFormat command. Make sure to employ Currency Style where appropriate, and do not allow this formatting to be overwritten by an AutoFormat. Print the worksheet and save the file as Solved-HR3.xls.

3. Open Solved-Rest2.xls, the other file you saved at the end of the previous lesson. Delete the column that holds the data for the average hours worked per day by each member of the waitstaff. Delete all of the labels that refer to days of the week in the schedule and replace them using an AutoFill. Apply bold formatting to all column heading labels and make their text green. Italicize all row heading labels and change their font to 11 point, Arial Narrow text. Define all horizontal ranges using the Name Box, and vertical ranges using menu commands. Save the file as Solved-Rest3.xls and print a hard copy.

4 . Replicate the worksheet shown below to the best of your ability.

Then, delete Column B, insert a row between the numbers section and the days section, insert three rows between the days section and the red pattern section, and finally, delete the extra cells that were added to Column A. Print the resulting worksheet.

L E S S O N

INSERTING OBJECTS AND CHARTS

Though the labels and values you enter into a spreadsheet serve as its core, other objects may represent certain data better or simply illustrate it further. Inserting these objects can break up the monotony of row after row of numbers and allow you to explain or highlight aspects of your spreadsheet that might otherwise go unnoticed.

You can insert a number of objects into your worksheet for the purpose of annotating specific information. These include text boxes, shapes such as arrows and connectors, and comments. Text boxes can be any size, but will obscure the portions of the worksheet behind them. Comments are similar to text boxes, but can be hidden from view. All graphics can be formatted and manipulated in a variety of ways.

One very effective way of enhancing your worksheet visually is to add a chart. The Chart Wizard can guide you through the process of creating a graphical representation of a data series that you select from your Excel worksheet. Charts can be moved, resized, and formatted. You can even change a chart's type and characteristics after it has been created. In addition, individual chart elements can be customized for emphasis and clarity.

CASE STUDY
In this lesson, Kay will strengthen her spreadsheet by inserting graphics and creating a chart using the Chart Wizard. Afterward, she will use some of Excel's advanced printing features to print a new copy of her worksheet.

Inserting Text Boxes

Concept

Text can also be inserted into a worksheet within a text box. Creating text boxes allows you to add passages of any size and appearance without the constraints of a cell in the worksheet. A text box is an independent object. Therefore, you can use it to reference data without affecting the data.

Do It!

Kay wants to insert a text box into her worksheet to emphasize the growth in projected Quarter 4 sales.

1 Click View, highlight Toolbars, then click Drawing if it is not already checked. The Drawing toolbar will be visible.

2 Click the Text Box button 🖾 on the Drawing toolbar. The pointer will change to the text cursor ↓ when it is in the workspace, allowing you to create a text box.

3 Click in cell E6, just below the green line where you want the top right corner of the text box to appear, then drag down and to the right to cell F7, until the box you have created is approximately one cell long by two cells high, like the one shown in **Figure 4-1**. When you release the mouse button, the borders of the box will become dotted and eight small squares called sizing handles will appear. There will be a sizing handle at each corner and one in the center of each side of the text box. A blinking insertion point will also appear in the text box.

4 Type Up 33% from Quarter 1 to enter it into the text box.

5 Click elsewhere in the worksheet to deselect the text box. Your worksheet should now resemble the one shown in **Figure 4-2**.

6 Save your worksheet.

More

The primary advantage of using text boxes is their flexibility. Text boxes may be easily moved, resized, or reformatted, without affecting the appearance or content of any other part of the worksheet. When text is being entered, a text box acts as a small word processing window. If there is not enough room on a line to fit a word, the text will wrap and continue on the next line. If the text box you have made is not large enough to accommodate the text as you are entering it, then the text will scroll upward, without changing the size or location of the box, to allow the additional text to be entered. The text box will have to be enlarged manually to view all of the text it contains. This can be accomplished through the use of the sizing handles, by clicking and dragging the handle in the desired direction of movement, expanding or reducing the size of the box.

Once a text box has been created, it is not fixed in place, but may be moved anywhere on the worksheet. To move a text box to another part of the worksheet, click the frame of a selected text box (not on a sizing handle) to select its frame, and then drag the text box to the desired destination.

Figure 4-1 Creating a text box

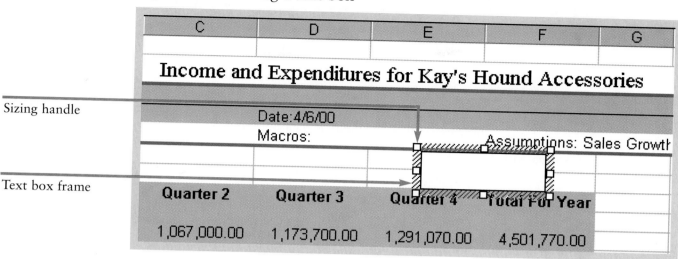

Sizing handle

Text box frame

Figure 4-2 Text box with text

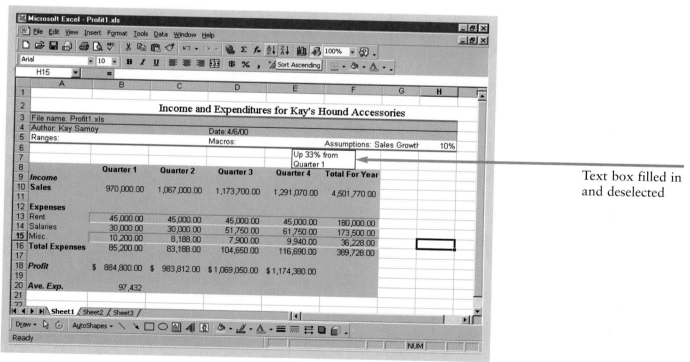

Text box filled in
and deselected

Practice

To practice inserting text boxes, open the practice file **Practice–Lesson 4.xls**, save the file as **MyPractice 4.xls**, then follow the instructions on the **Prac4-1** tab.

Hot Tip

Text boxes are always visible, and hide the portion of the worksheet behind them. Text boxes can overlap each other, however, and their order can be changed by right-clicking one and choosing an option from the Order submenu that appears.

Enhancing Graphics

Concept

Graphic objects that you have inserted, such as lines, text boxes, or pictures, can be modified to alter and improve their appearance.

Do It!

Kay will add a callout arrow and color to the text box that she inserted in the previous Skill.

1. Click the Arrow button 🖾 on the Drawing toolbar. It will indent, and the mouse pointer will appear as a thin cross + when it is over the worksheet.

2. Position the pointer just after the **1** in the text box, then click and drag to cell E10, the Sales value for Quarter 4. When the mouse button is released, the line that was being drawn becomes fixed, and an arrowhead appears at the end.

3. Click the text box to select it. Its frame becomes a thick hatched line.

4. Click the text box's frame (but not a sizing handle) to select the frame. It changes from a hatched to a dotted border.

5. Click the arrow on the Fill Color button 🖾 on the drawing toolbar to open the Fill Color palette.

6. Click the pale blue square in the bottom row of the palette to select it. The text box's background will change to match the selected color.

7. Click the arrow you drew to select it. A sizing handle appears at each end of the arrow to indicate its selection.

8. Click the Line Color drop-down arrow 🖾 to open the Line Color palette, and select the red square in the middle of the first column. The arrow will change to match the color of the selected square.

9. Click elsewhere in the worksheet to deselect the arrow. The text box and arrow should now resemble the ones shown in **Figure 4-3**.

More

The Format menu is context-sensitive, which means that its content changes based on the item that is selected. When a cell is active, the Format menu contains commands for altering a cell, while a selected AutoShape will cause another set of commands to appear on the Format menu. Objects that are inserted into an Excel document, such as lines, AutoShapes, and Clip Art, all have their own formatting dialog boxes with tabs relating to the selected object.

The Format Text Box command, available on the Format menu when a text box is selected, opens the Format Text Box dialog box shown in **Figure 4-4**. This dialog box contains seven tabs with options for altering many aspects of a text box. While many of the controls found in the Format Text Box dialog box have toolbar buttons, the dialog box allows more precise and comprehensive control over such aspects the size of the text box, the internal margins of the text box, and the orientation of text within a text box.

Figure 4-3 Enhancing worksheet graphics

Text box with blue
background

Inserted red arrow

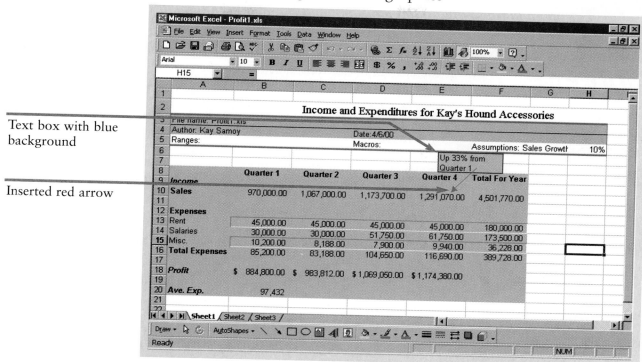

Excel 2000

Figure 4-4 Format Text Box dialog box

Click a tab to format
the corresponding
aspect of the selected
text box

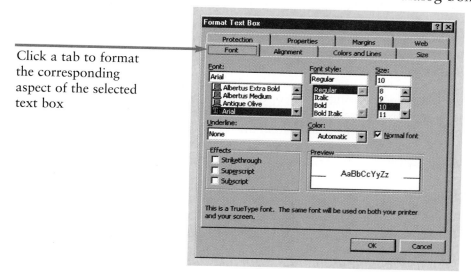

Practice

To practice enhancing graphics follow the
instructions on the **Prac4-2** tab of the practice file **MyPractice 4.xls**.

Hot Tip

You can open an object's formatting dialog
box by double-clicking it. Double-clicking a
text box's frame will open the dialog box
shown above, but double-clicking in the
text box will only allow you to alter the text
itself.

 # Adding Comments

Concept

A comment is an electronic note that can be attached to a cell. Comments are hidden from view until the mouse pointer is over a cell that contains one. Comments are useful for documenting information or making notes. If multiple people will be using a spreadsheet, comments can be used as a way to share information.

Do It!

Since there is not enough room in the documentation section of her worksheet to list all of the named ranges, Kay will insert a comment containing the range names.

1. Click cell A5 to make it active.

2. Click Insert, then click Comment. An active text box with the name of the designated user and an insertion point, shown in Figure 4-5, will appear next to the selected cell. The text box will have an arrow pointing to the cell it references and a red triangle will appear in the upper-right corner of the cell indicating that it contains a comment.

3. Select the contents of the cell by dragging the I-beam over the text in the box.

4. Type Kay Samoy: and then press [Enter]. This is to indicate that Kay is the author of the comment. Notice that the name that first appeared in the comment box appears in the status bar. This can be changed from the General tab of the Options dialog box available on the Tools menu.

5. Type the following range names, pressing [Enter] after each: Miscellaneous, Profit, Quarter 1, Quarter 2, Quarter 3, Quarter 4, Rent, Salaries, Sales, Total Expenses. The text will scroll as you type hiding the first few entries.

6. Drag the midpoint sizing handle of the bottom edge of the comment box down until it is approximately even with row 13. When you release the mouse button the comment box will expand so that all the text will be visible as shown in Figure 4-6.

7. Click elsewhere in the worksheet to deselect cell A5 and hide the comment.

8. Position the pointer over cell A5. The comment will be displayed.

9. Save your workbook.

More

Like cells and text boxes, comment boxes and the text they contain can be formatted. Right-clicking a cell that contains a comment opens a pop-up menu with a command for editing and deleting comments. These commands activate the comment connected to the selected cell. Double-clicking the comment's border will open the Format Comment dialog box, and clicking in the comment box will allow you to manipulated the text itself. The Reviewing toolbar, whose buttons are listed in Table 4-1, contains commands for displaying and navigating among comments. It can be activated from the Toolbars submenu on the View menu. Once a comment has been opened for editing, you can move it anywhere in the worksheet by clicking and dragging its border; a line will always run from the comment to its parent cell.

Figure 4-5 Adding a comment to a cell

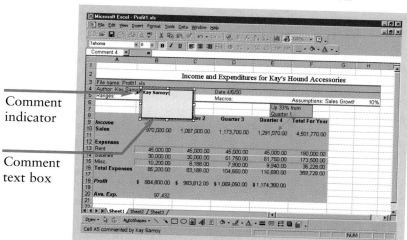

Comment indicator

Comment text box

Figure 4-6 Kay's comment

Kay Samoy:
Miscellaneous
Profit
Quarter 1
Quarter 2
Quarter 3
Quarter 4
Rent
Salaries
Sales
Total Expenses

Excel 2000

Table 4-1 Reviewing toolbar buttons

BUTTON	NAME	FUNCTION
	New Comment	Opens a new comment
	Edit Comment	Displays the comment with an insertion point in the comment pane
	Previous Comment	Displays the previous comment
	Next Comment	Displays the next comment
	Show/Hide Comment	Leaves a comment visible even when the mouse pointer is not over the selected parent cell; deselecting this button returns the comment to its default hidden state
	Show/Hide All Comments	Shows or hides all comments on the worksheet
	Delete Comment	Permanently removes a comment and its reference mark in the parent cell

Practice

To practice adding comments, follow the instructions on the **Prac4-3** tab of the practice file **MyPractice 4.xls**.

Hot Tip

Either the New Comment button or the Edit Comment button will appear on the Reviewing toolbar, depending on whether or not the selected cell already contains a comment.

Creating a Chart

Concept

Charts are graphics that represent values and their relationships. Using charts you can quickly identify trends in data, and see the contrasts among values. Excel allows you to portray data easily using a variety of two- and three-dimensional chart styles. These styles give data immediate meaning, unlike data in its raw form, which generally requires studying.

Do It!

Kay wants to show the values for Rent, Salaries, and Miscellaneous expenses as percentages of her total yearly expenses.

1. Select the range F13:F15. These are the values that are required to create the chart.

2. Click the Chart Wizard button on the Standard toolbar. The Chart Wizard dialog box opens, as shown in **Figure 4-7**, with the Column chart type selected. If the Office Assistant appears, close it by clicking the No, I do not want help now option as the Assistant is not necessary for this Skill.

3. Click Pie in the Chart type list box. The Chart sub-types will change to show different type of pie charts.

4. Click Next >. The Wizard will advance to its second step with a pie chart representing the selected data displayed. If you had not already selected cells you could enter which cells to include in your chart in the data range text box.

5. Click the Series tab to bring it the front of the stack.

6. Click the Category Labels text box to activate it. A flashing insertion point will appear in the text box so you can name the categories for you chart.

7. Click the Collapse Dialog button. The dialog box will shrink so only the Category Labels text box is shown. Collapsing the dialog box allows you to view more of the worksheet so you can easily select the cells to be inserted as the labels for your chart's categories.

8. Select A13:A15. An animated border will surround the selected range, a ScreenTip will display the size of the selection, and the range will appear in the collapsed dialog box, as shown in **Figure 4-8**.

Figure 4-7 Chart Wizard dialog box: Step 1

Click here to select a chart type

Click here to select a chart sub-type

Name and description of the selected chart sub-type

Click here to to preview the chart sub-type using data extracted from your worksheet

Excel 2000

Figure 4-8   Selecting the category labels

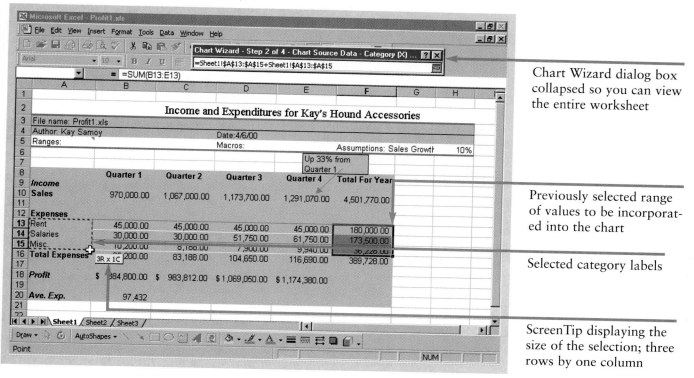

Chart Wizard dialog box collapsed so you can view the entire worksheet

Previously selected range of values to be incorporated into the chart

Selected category labels

ScreenTip displaying the size of the selection; three rows by one column

Creating
a Chart (continued)

Do It!

9   Click the Expand Dialog button 🖻 to bring the full dialog box into view.

10   Click Next > . The third step of the Wizard will be shown.

11   Click the Chart tile text box, then type Breakdown of Expenses. The title you have entered will appear in the preview area to the right of the text box. The other other text boxes are grayed out since they are not applicable to the chosen chart type.

12   Click the Legend tab to bring it to the front of the stack.

13   Click the Show legend check box to deselect this option, as you will be labeling the chart later.

14   Click the Data Labels tab to bring it to the front of the stack.

15   Click the Show label and percent radio button. Labels and percentages will appear in the preview.

16   Click Next > to advance to the last step of the Wizard. As you can see in **Figure 4-9**, the As object in radio button is selected, indicating that the chart will appear in the current worksheet as opposed to a new one.

17   Click Finish . The Chart Wizard dialog box will close, your chart will be displayed in the center of your worksheet, and the Chart toolbar will appear in the Excel window, as shown in **Figure 4-10**.

18   Save your workbook.

More

When the chart is selected, the Data menu is replaced by the Chart menu. The first four commands on the Chart menu open dialog boxes that are similar to the steps of the Chart Wizard. This allows you to alter any of the characteristics of the chart without having to recreate it with the Chart Wizard. The Add Data command lets you append the ranges that are displayed.

Figure 4-9 Chart Wizard dialog box: Step 4

Click to create chart in its own, new worksheet

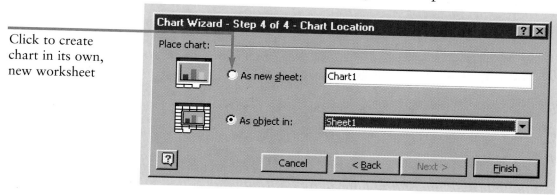

Figure 4-10 Finished chart

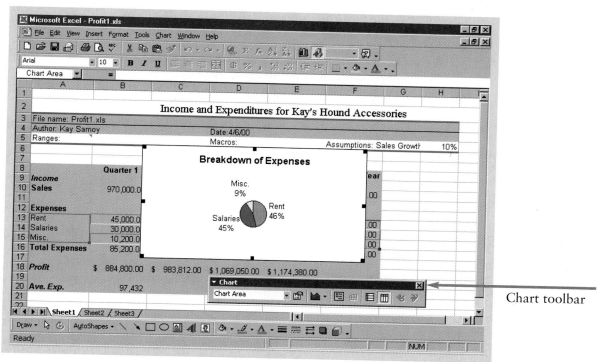

Chart toolbar

Practice

To practice creating a chart, follow the instructions on the **Prac4-4** tab of the practice file **MyPractice 4.xls**.

Hot Tip

When a chart is selected, ranges that it references will be selected in the worksheet. You can add or subtract cells from the ranges portrayed in the chart by dragging a selected range's fill handle. Moving the cell pointer selects a new range.

 # Moving and Resizing a Chart

Concept

Once you have created a chart, you can change its size and location in the work-sheet so that it complements your data without obstructing it. While a chart may be the focus of your worksheet, it is still just one part of the overall presentation.

Do It!

Kay wants to move the chart below the main data of her worksheet and then resize it so that its boundaries match those of existing columns and rows.

1. Click the selected chart and drag it down and to the left until the upper-left corner of the dotted border is in cell A21 (see **Figure 4-11**). As you move the mouse the pointer will change to the movement pointer ✛ and the dotted border will indicate where the chart will appear when the mouse button is released. The worksheet will scroll upward when the mouse pointer is dragged below the document window.

2. Scroll downward until the entire chart can be seen in the document window, if it is not already.

3. Position the mouse pointer over the midpoint sizing handle of the right edge of the chart, then click and drag the edge of the chart to the left until it is even with the boundary between columns C and D. The chart will adjust itself so it remains centered and proportional in its box.

4. Using the midpoint sizing handle on the bottom of the chart, drag the chart edge to the boundary between rows 34 and 35. Notice that the chart elements expand slightly to fill the larger area. Your chart should resemble the one shown in **Figure 4-11**.

5. Save your workbook.

More

Table 4-2 below summarizes different techniques you can use to move and resize charts and other objects.

Table 4-2 Object resizing techniques

ACTION	TO
Press [Shift] while dragging the chart	Constrain a chart's movement to only the horizontal or vertical
Press [Ctrl] while dragging the chart	Copy the chart to another place in the worksheet
Press [Shift] while dragging a corner sizing handle	Constrain a chart's aspect ratio when resizing it
Press [Ctrl] while dragging a sizing handle	Maintain a chart's center point when resizing
Press [Ctrl]+[Shift] while dragging a corner sizing handle	Maintain a chart's center point and aspect ratio when resizing

Figure 4-11 Repositioned and resized chart

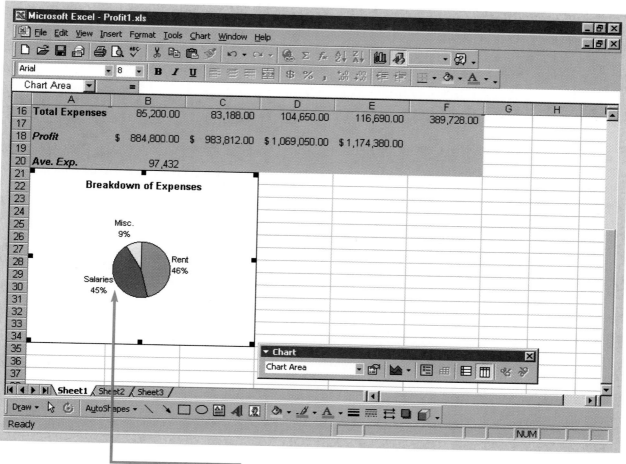

Chart elements adjust
to fit the redefined
chart area

Excel 2000

Practice

To practice moving and resizing a chart,
follow the instructions on the **Prac4-5** tab
of the practice file **MyPractice 4.xls**.

Hot Tip

As you move the mouse pointer over various elements of the chart, ScreenTips will
appear with a brief explanation of that
item. These ScreenTips may be disabled by
pressing [Alt].

EX 4.13

Formatting a Chart

Concept

After a chart has been created, many of its features may be altered. The color and location of chart elements can be changed, and formatting can be applied to text.

Do It!

Kay wants to emphasize that her company has met its goal of keeping miscellaneous expenses under of 10% of total expenses by isolating the corresponding pie slice in the chart and changing its color. She would also like to format the chart title.

1. Click the pie in your chart to make it active. Three sizing handles will appear indicating its selection.

2. Click the Miscellaneous pie slice to select it.

3. Click and drag the Miscellaneous slice away from the pie so the point of the triangle is even with the former border of the pie. Notice that the slice's label moves to accommodate the slice's new position. (See **Figure 4-13**.)

4. Double-click the Miscellaneous pie slice. The Format Data Point dialog box opens.

5. Click the Patterns tab, shown in **Figure 4-12**, to bring it to front if it is not already there.

6. In the Area section of the tab, click the yellow box in the bottom row, beneath the currently selected color. The sample color, shown in the lower left of the tab, will change to illustrate the newly selected color.

7. Click [OK]. The dialog box closes, and the chart will appear with the new color applied to the Miscellaneous slice, as seen in **Figure 4-13**.

8. Double-click the chart's title, Breakdown of Expenses, to open the Format Chart Title dialog box.

9. On the Patterns tab, click the Shadow check box to activate it.

10. Click [OK]. The dialog box closes, and the chart's title now appears in a box with a shadow applied to it. Click elsewhere in the worksheet to deselect the chart title; your chart should now resemble the one shown in **Figure 4-13**.

More

Double-clicking any element of a chart will open a dialog box that enables you to format and alter the selected chart element. Depending upon what item is selected, the available tabs of this dialog box will provide the appropriate formatting options. Elements may also be selected and their formatting dialog boxes opened using the Chart toolbar, pictured in **Figure 4-14**.

On the Patterns tab of chart element formatting dialog boxes there is a Fill Effects button that lets you apply advanced formatting options such as gradients, textures, patterns, or pictures to the selected element.

Figure 4-12 Format Data Point dialog box

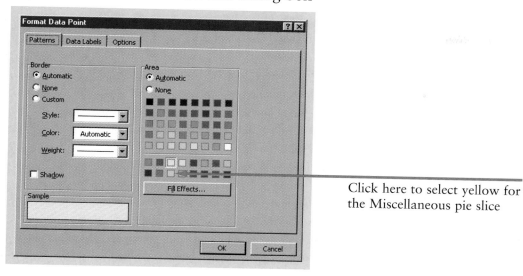

Click here to select yellow for the Miscellaneous pie slice

Figure 4-13 Formatted chart elements

Chart title formatted with a shadow

Miscellaneous slice with new color and dragged away from the pie

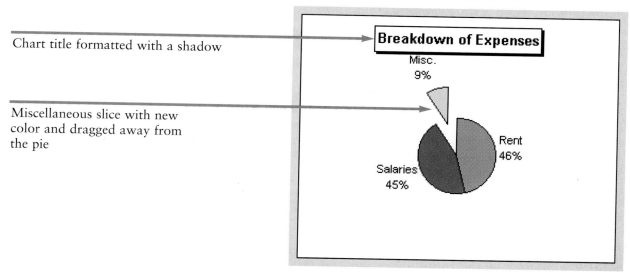

Figure 4-14 Chart toolbar

Practice

To practice formatting a chart, follow the instructions on the **Prac4-6** tab of the practice file **MyPractice 4.xls**.

Hot Tip

Chart titles and labels may be dragged to new locations in the chart area, as can the chart itself.

Changing a Chart's Type

Concept

Excel allows you to change a chart's type while maintaining the same referenced data series. For example, a bar chart can be easily converted to a line graph to more effectively present the data it contains. You may also switch between variants of the same chart type, called sub-types, that will make your chart easier to read.

Do It!

Kay would like to display her pie chart with a 3-D visual effect.

1 With the chart selected, click Chart, then click Chart Type. The Chart Type dialog box opens with the Standard Types tab in front, with the selected chart's type and sub-type selected (if the Standard Types tab is not in front, click it now).

2 Click the second chart sub-type, Pie with a 3-D visual effect. It will become highlighted, and a description of it will appear in the area beneath the Chart sub-types.

3 Click [OK]. The dialog box closes, and your chart appears with the new sub-type applied, as shown in **Figure 4-15**.

4 Click Chart, then click 3-D View. The 3-D View dialog box, shown in **Figure 4-16**, appears with the current elevation of 15 degrees selected.

5 Click [⬆] twice to increase the chart's elevation to 25 degrees. The chart in the preview box will pivot, illustrating the effect that the changes you are making will have on the chart.

6 Click [OK]. The dialog box closes and the chart reflects the changes that you have made, as shown in **Figure 4-17**. Save your changes.

More

Table 4-3 Chart types

CHART TYPE	DESCRIPTION	EXAMPLE
Column	Data changes over time or quantitative comparisons among items	Quarterly income projections
Bar	Similar to a column chart, but horizontal orientation places more value on the X value	Individual sales performance
Line	Trends in data at fixed intervals	Tracking stock trends
Pie	The percentage each value contributes to the whole. Used for a single data series	Budgets, chief exports of a country
XY (Scatter)	Comparative relationships between seemingly dissimilar data	Scientific data analysis
Surface	The range of intersections between two sets of data	Optimal fuel consumption

Figure 4-15 Pie with a 3-D visual effect

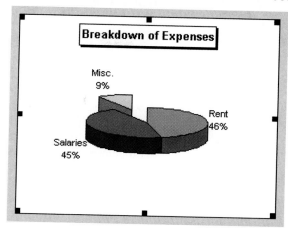

Figure 4-16 Chart toolbar

Click here to increase or decrease chart elevation below

Click to revert to chart's original elevation and rotation

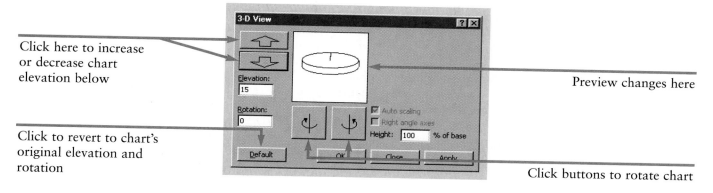

Preview changes here

Click buttons to rotate chart

Figure 4-17 Chart with increased elevation

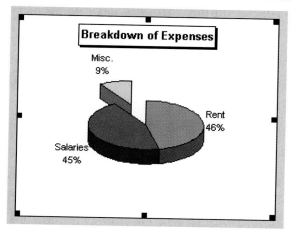

Practice

To practice changing a chart's type, follow the instructions on the **Prac4-7** tab of **MyPractice 4.xls**.

Hot Tip

The Chart Type drop-down arrow on the Chart toolbar allows you to quickly change the selected chart from one type to another.

 # Using Advanced Printing Features

Concept

A worksheet, especially one that contains embedded objects such as a chart, may not always fit on a standard printed page using the default printing settings. Excel allows you to preview and change page orientation so as to accommodate different arrangements of data. You can also choose to print specific parts of a spreadsheet such as a chart, a page, the active worksheet, or the entire workbook. As in many programs, you can access these options through the Page Setup dialog box and the Print dialog box. Using these dialog boxes in conjuntion with the Print Preview will allow you to get the most out of printing your work.

Do It!

Kay wants to change the page orientation so her entire worksheet will fit onto one printed page.

1. Click outside of the chart to deselect it.

2. Click the Print Preview button 🔍. Your worksheet will be displayed in Print Preview mode. Notice that the status bar reads Preview: Page 1 of 2, and the Next button is active indicating that there is another page.

3. Click in the upper-right corner of the document preview with the magnification pointer. As you can see from **Figure 4-18**, the worksheet will appear magnified in the window with the worksheet title and cell labels cropped, making it apparent that the entire worksheet does not fit on the page.

4. Click Setup... . The Page Setup dialog box will appear as shown in **Figure 4-19**.

5. Click the Landscape radio button in the Orientation section of the dialog box.

6. Click OK . The dialog box will close and you will see that the entire worksheet is now visible on the preview page.

Figure 4-18 Magnified worksheet in Print Preview

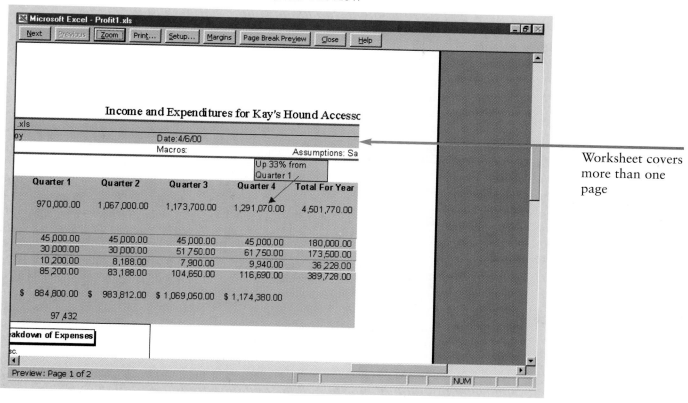

Worksheet covers
more than one
page

Figure 4-19 Page Setup dialog box

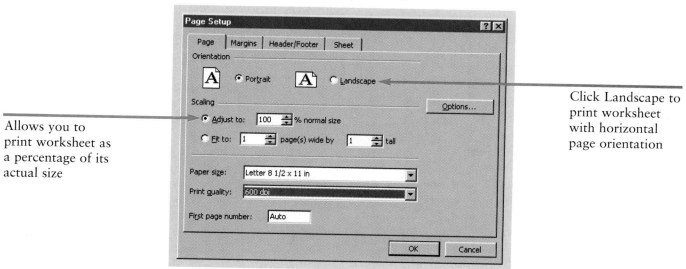

Allows you to
print worksheet as
a percentage of its
actual size

Click Landscape to
print worksheet
with horizontal
page orientation

Using Advanced Printing Features

(continued)

Do It!

7 Click the preview to zoom out. The entire page will appear horizontally in the window but the status bar will still read Page 1 of 2, as shown in **Figure 4-20** (if this is not the case, exit Print Preview, change the widths of columns A through H to at least 14 characters, and then return to Print Preview and continue).

8 Click Next . A blank page appears. This is page contains blank cells that belong to cell A2 which was merged to encompass the range A2:J2 when the title was centered. It is not necessary to print this second page as it only contains blank cells.

9 Click Print... . Print Preview will close, you will be returned to normal view, and the Print dialog box will open.

10 In the Print range section of the dialog box, click the up arrow of the From text box. A 1 will appear selected in the box designating it as the first page to print, and the Page(s) radio button will be selected.

11 Click the up arrow in the To text box. A 1 will appear selected in the box telling Excel to stop printing after page 1.

12 Click OK . The Print dialog box will close and the document will be sent to the printer.

13 Save your workbook.

More

Excel's print function allows you select the area or item you wish to print. Therefore, you do not have to send an entire worksheet to the printer if you wish to have a hard copy of a smaller portion. With a chart selected, the Print dialog box will have the Selected Chart radio button active in the Print what area so that only the chart, and not the remaining data of the worksheet, will be printed. Likewise, the Print Preview will display just the chart, as this view shows you exactly how the information will be printed with the current settings. If you select a chart, then click the Page Setup command found on the File menu, the Page Setup dialog box will open with a tab labeled Chart. Compare this dialog box shown in **Figure 4-21** to the one shown in **Figure 4-19**. This tab contains options concerning the chart's printed size and print quality.

Figure 4-20 Preview of worksheet in landscape orientation

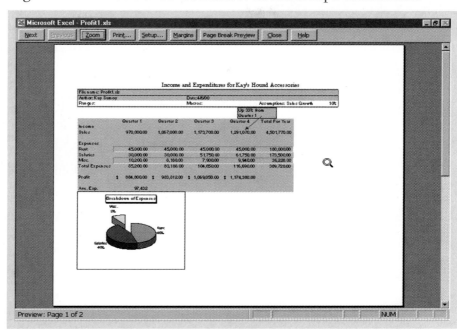

Excel 2000

Figure 4-21 Page Setup dialog box when a chart is selected

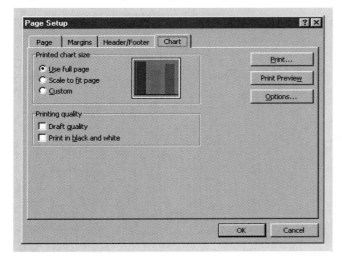

Practice

To practice using advanced printing features, follow the instructions on the **Prac4-
8** tab of the practice file **MyPractice 4.xls**.

Hot Tip

The Page Break Preview command, found
on the View menu, allows you to adjust
what portion of the worksheet will fit on
one printed page. The data contained in the
worksheet will be reduced to fit on the
page if you expand the print range.

Shortcuts

Function	Button/Mouse	Menu	Keyboard
Drawing toolbar		Click View, then highlight Toolbars, then click Drawing	
Chart Wizard		Click Insert, then click Chart	
Format chart area (or selected chart object)		Click Format, then click Selected Chart Area (or other object)	[Ctrl]+[1]
Change chart type		Click Chart, then click Chart Type	
Add/Remove chart legend		Click Chart, then click Chart Options	
Plot chart data series by row		Click Chart, then click Source Data	
Plot chart data series by column		Click Chart, then click Source Data	

Identify Key Features

Name the items indicated by callouts in **Figure 4-22**.

Figure 4-22 Identify features of the Excel screen

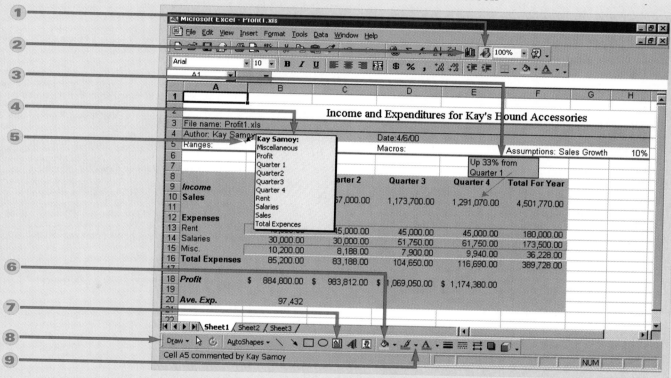

Excel 2000

Select The Best Answer

10. Allows you to add text to a worksheet without worrying about cell constraints

11. Reduces the size of a dialog box so that you can easily view the worksheet

12. Appears along with your chart when you complete the Chart Wizard

13. Allows you to format any chart element from a dialog box

14. Indicates that a chart will be printed as opposed to the entire worksheet

15. An electronic note attached to a cell

16. A graphic that represents values and their relationships

17. Horizontal page orientation

18. Allows you to add colors and gradients to chart elements

a. Collapse dialog button

b. Double-clicking

c. Patterns tab

d. Chart toolbar

e. Selected Chart radio button

f. Landscape

g. Text box

h. Comment

i. Chart

Quiz (continued)

Complete the Statement

19. To change the user name that appears on comments, go to the:

    a. Summary tab in the Properties dialog box

    b. Replace dialog box

    c. Define Name dialog box

    d. General tab in the Options dialog box

20. The Arrow tool can be found on the:

    a. Standard toolbar

    b. Formatting toolbar

    c. Drawing toolbar

    d. Shapes toolbar

21. To navigate among comments, use the:

    a. Comment toolbar

    b. Reviewing toolbar

    c. Standard toolbar

    d. Vertical scroll bar

22. All of the following are standard chart types except:

    a. Pie

    b. Doughnut

    c. Line

    d. Volume

23. You can add a title to a chart by using the:

    a. Chart Options dialog box

    b. Source Data dialog box

    c. Format Chart area dialog box

    d. Chart Type dialog box

24. You may change all of the following chart aspects from the 3-D View dialog box with the exception of:

    a. Elevation

    b. Rotation

    c. Height

    d. Location

25. To maintain a chart's center point when resizing it:

    a. Press [Ctrl] while dragging the chart

    b. Press [Shift] while dragging a sizing handle

    c. Press [Ctrl] while dragging a sizing handle

    d. Press [Tab] while dragging a sizing handle

26. If the text in a text box exceeds the size of the box:

    a. The text box will resize itself

    b. The beginning of the text will be deleted

    c. The text will scroll up

    d. No more text can be added.

27. The small squares in the corners and middle of each side of a comment or chart are called:

    a. Sizing handles

    b. Fill handles

    c. Jug handles

    d. Frames

Interactivity

Test Your Skills

1. Add objects and graphics to a spreadsheet:

   a. Open the file Test 3.xls that you created at the end of the previous Lesson.

   b. Add a text box that says Best day for relaxation and errands above the day of the week column of your choice.

   c. Use the Fill Color palette to add color to the text box.

   d. Draw an arrow from the text box to the appropriate day of the week label.

   e. Use the Line Color palette to add color to the arrow.

   f. Enter a comment that displays the names of all your defined ranges in the cell that contains the Ranges label.

2. Create a chart based on your worksheet data:

   a. Select the Average range in your worksheet by using the Name Box.

   b. Use the Chart Wizard to create a basic pie chart that plots each daily activity as a percentage of the total time you spend on all of your activities during an average day.

   c. In Step 2 of the Wizard, use the Series tab to select the appropriate Category Labels for your chart.

   d. In Step 3, choose a title for the chart, leave the legend displayed on the right, and show percent data labels.

   e. In Step 4, insert the chart into the current worksheet.

3. Move, resize, and format a chart:

   a. Move the chart so that it is centered below the data portion of the worksheet.

   b. Adjust the borders of the chart and the legend so that no chart elements obscure each other. Make any other size and placement adjustments that you think will improve the appearance of the chart.

   c. Change the chart's sub-type to a 3-D Exploded pie.

   d. Increase the elevation of the pie by thirty degrees, and rotate it twenty degrees counter-clockwise.

   e. Change the color of the largest pie slice in the chart.

   f. Add a shadow to your chart's title and fill the title box with color.

4. Save and print the changes you have made to the spreadsheet:

   a. Save the file as Test 4.xls.

   b. Preview the worksheet and use the Page Setup dialog box to make it fit on one page if necessary.

   c. Print a copy of the entire worksheet.

   d. Print a copy of just the chart.

Interactivity (continued)

Problem Solving

1. A friend of yours is considering learning Microsoft Excel. You want to convince your friend that the task is well worthwhile. In order to do this, you plan to show him or her the spreadsheets you have created while learning Excel. First, however, you decide to incorporate the latest techniques you have learned into the spreadsheets so that they are truly impressive. Return to the files Solved 2.xls and Solved 3-Grad.xls, and add at least one text box, one comment, and a chart to each. Use these features to call attention to and further illustrate important data in the worksheets. Be sure to save the additions you make to the files. Save the files as Solved 4.xls and Solved 4-Grad.xls.

2. Open the file Solved-HR3.xls, which you saved at the end of the previous lesson. Using the data you have already entered, create a 3D Pie chart to express graphically the distribution of the $10,000 that has been added to your Human Resources expense account. Also, add a text box that explains that the figures are proposals based on your preferences and projections. Then add two arrows – one that points from the text box to the chart, and one that points from the text box to the actual data. Print the worksheet and save the file as Solved-HR4.xls.

3. Open the file Solved-Rest3.xls, which you also saved at the end of the previous lesson. Insert a comment in the worksheet that lists all the ranges that the worksheet contains (if you do not have a cell labeled Ranges, add one and then insert the comment in this cell). Format the comment so that its background is Sky Blue and its text is Red. Then, add data to the worksheet, including appropriate labels and values, that details the pay scale at the restaurant. For example, include the pay rate earned by an employee with 0-6 months experience, 6-12 months experience, 12-18 months experience, etc. Finally, use the Chart Wizard to express this data with a Bar chart (use the Clustered Bar sub-type). Save the file as Solved-Rest4.xls and print a copy of just the chart.

4. Use Excel to create the worksheet below. You will need to make formatting changes to the chart once it is created.

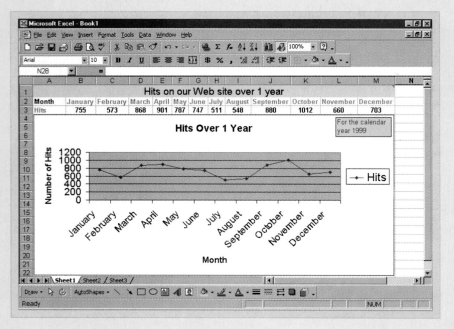

When you are finished, change the chart type to Stacked Column. Format the axis and series labels so that they are easy to read. Decide which chart type presents the data more effectively and keep that chart in the worksheet, changing back to the original if necessary. Save your file as Solved4-Hits.xls.

L E S S O N

USING MACROS

When working with a spreadsheet, you may find yourself doing the same thing, or using the same commands repeatedly. One of the more convenient features of Excel 2000 is the macro. A macro is a set of instructions that executes commands in a specified order. Macros allow you to automate many of the commands that you use. For example, you can create a macro that removes the gridlines from the active worksheet. Normally, removing the gridlines from a worksheet is a multistep process. However, a macro reduces the operation to one step.

Careful planning is essential in the creation of a macro. It would be best to outline the commands your macro will perform so you can achieve the desired results.

A macro is created by recording a series of commands and keystrokes as they would normally be performed in the course of completing the necessary actions. As you record a macro, each action is translated into programming code that you can later view and modify. Once a macro is recorded it can be played back at any time to perform the recorded commands in one step. If the macro does not work exactly as you planned, it can be edited so as to remove or add functionality. A macro can be added to a toolbar as a button or to a menu as a command.

Case Study:
Kay will be creating a macro to calculate estimated sales growth in different increments to see how it will affect the rest of her worksheet.

Recording a Macro

Concept

Once you have figured out what steps you would like your macro to perform, you are ready to begin recording it. Recording a macro is easy using the Macro recorder function in Excel.

Do It!

Kay will record a macro that prints out five copies of her worksheet, each with a different value for projected sales growth.

1. Open the file named Doit5-1.xls from your student folder and save it as Profit2.xls.

2. Click Tools, then rest the pointer over Macros until the submenu opens. Click Record New Macro. The Record Macro dialog box appears, as shown in **Figure 5-1**.

3. Type Sales_Projection to name the macro. Be sure to include the underscore ([Shift]+[-]), since macro names cannot contain any spaces.

4. Click the Shortcut key text box, then type [m]. This allows you to run the macro by pressing [Ctrl]+[m].

5. Click to the right of Samoy in the Description text box, then press [Enter] to begin a new line.

6. Type changes sales growth figure and prints the page to add it to the macro's description.

7. Click [OK]. The Record Macro dialog box will close, the Stop Recording toolbar opens (if it does not, select Stop Recording from the Toolbars submenu on the View menu), and the status bar will read Ready Recording, indicating that you can begin recording your macro.

8. Click cell H5 to select it.

9. Type .05 to change the Sales Growth Assumption, click the Enter button [✓] to confirm the new entry (notice that the data in the worksheet is recalculated to reflect this change), then click the Print button [🖨] to send a copy of the newly calculated data to the printer.

10. Repeat the above step four times, substituting .10, .15, .20, and .25 for each Sales Growth assumption.

11. Click the Stop Recording button [■]. (see **Figure 5-2**). The Stop Recording toolbar will close. Your macro has been recorded.

12. Save your workbook.

More

By default, the macro recorder uses absolute cell references when it records. If you would like to use relative cell references in your macro, click the Relative Reference button ▦ on the Stop Recording toolbar before you select a cell. The button will remain depressed, indicating that the relative cell references are being recorded, until it is clicked again, to revert to absolute cell references.

Excel 2000

Figure 5-1 Record Macro dialog box

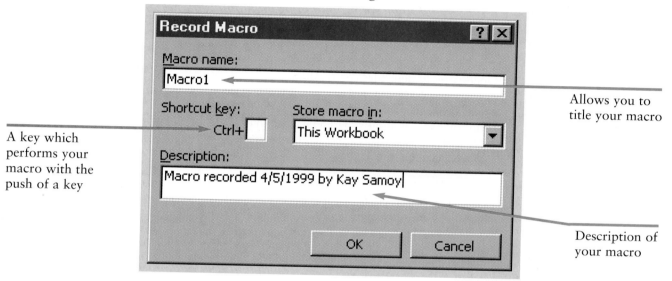

A key which performs your macro with the push of a key

Allows you to title your macro

Description of your macro

Figure 5-2 Stop Recording toolbar

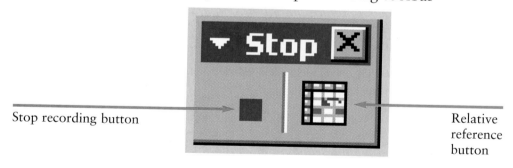

Stop recording button

Relative reference button

Practice

To practice recording a macro, open the Student practice file **Prac5-1.xls**, save it as **MyPractice5**, and then follow the instructions on the Prac5-1 sheet.

Hot Tip

You can take as much time as necessary to record a macro, without having to worry about pauses between the actions. **Excel** will play back the series of commands in succession without any pauses.

Running a Macro

Concept

Once you have recorded a macro, it can be run at any time in the workbook where it was created. It is always a good idea to test a macro you have recorded to ensure that it works as intended.

Do It!

Kay wants to run the macro she recorded in order to make sure that it was recorded correctly.

1. Open your student file MyPractice5.xls.

2. Click Tools, rest the pointer over Macros until the submenu opens. Select Macros from the Macros submenu. The Macro dialog box opens with the macro Sales_Projections selected in the macros field and appearing in the Macro name textbox, as shown in **Figure 5-3**. Be sure your computer is connected to a printer.

3. Click ▢ Run ▢. The Macro dialog box will close and the macro will be executed. If your macro ran correctly, five pages should have been sent to the printer with the data in cell H5 displaying 5 to 25% in five percent increments.

4. Click cell D5 to select it.

5. Click once in the formula bar, to the right of Macros:. A flashing insertion point will appear.

6. Type [Space], [Space], Sales_Projection to document your macro, then press [Enter]. Your worksheet should now look like the one shown in **Figure 5-4**.

7. Save your workbook.

More

The Macro dialog box offers several buttons that allow you to manipulate your macro. In the above exercise, you used the Run button to initiate your macro. The Cancel button closes the Macro dialog box and returns you to the active worksheet. The Step Into and Edit buttons open the Microsoft Visual Basic application which can be used to work with the actual code or programming language of the macro. Clicking the Step Into button opens the Visual Basic in debugging mode, allowing you to run the macro while pausing at predetermined points so you can ascertain where possible errors may be occurring. The Delete button erases the selected macro. The Options button opens the Macro Options dialog box, which lets you edit the macro's description and alter the shortcut key that runs the macro.

Excel 2000

Figure 5-3 Macro dialog box

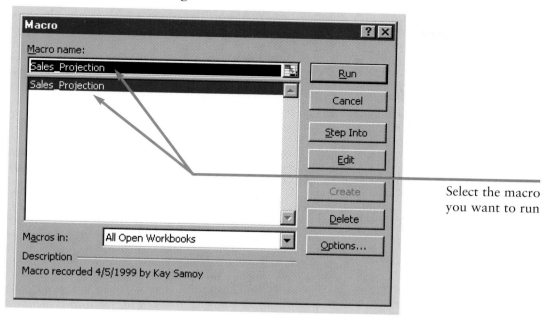

Select the macro
you want to run

Figure 5-4 Excel worksheet

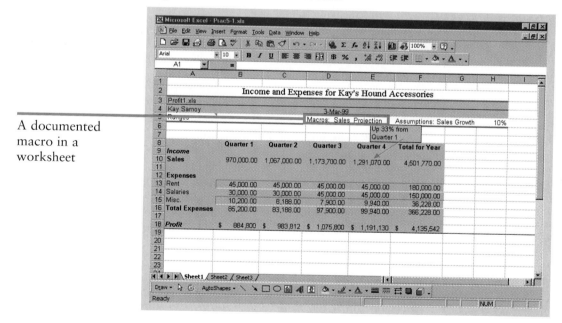

A documented
macro in a
worksheet

Practice

To practice running a macro, run the macro
that you created and saved as
MyPractice5.

Hot Tip

To stop a macro before it has finished
running, press **[Esc]**.

EX 5.5

Editing a Macro

Concept

If you would like to alter the function of a macro, you might think you have to rerecord it. That's one option, but there is a faster way. When a macro is first recorded, Excel keeps a record of each command and action that you undertake in programming code, which you can then view and manipulate using Microsoft Visual Basic. Though unwieldy for making major changes, the Edit Macro function can be very helpful when only small modifications are necessary.

Do It!

Kay wants to edit the macro she has created so that it will return to the worksheet in its original state when the macro is finished running.

1 Open the student file MyPractice5.xls.

2 Click Tools, rest the pointer over Macro until the submenu opens, and then click on Macro from the submenu. The Macro dialog box will open.

3 Click [Edit] to open Visual Basic. The Visual Basic window and its components are shown in **Figure 5-5**. Look over the steps of your macro, which should match those in the Profit2.xls-Module1 (Code) window. Each line corresponds with an action that was taken when the macro was recorded.

4 Select the fifth line in the main body of the macro, as shown in **Figure 5-5**. This line of code instructs Excel to change the contents of the active cell to 10%.

5 Click Edit, then click Copy to send a copy of this line of code to the Clipboard.

6 Click once after the last line in the main body of the Macro Code then press [Enter]. The insertion point should now be located in a blank line above the End Sub heading.

7 Click Edit, then click Paste to insert the copied line of code into the macro at the insertion point. With this new line of code inserted, the original value of 10% will be restored as the sales growth assumption when the macro has finished running. Your macro codes should now match that shown in **Figure 5-6**.

8 Click [X] at the upper-right of the Microsoft Visual Basic window to close it and return to the worksheet.

9 Save your worksheet to incorporate the changes you have made to the macro.

More

You may easily undo an action that you have made by accident, by clicking Edit, then Undo. This command will undo the very last action which you performed. If you decide you want to perform the action again, you may click Edit, then Redo to perform the action you had previously undone.

Figure 5-5 Visual Basic window

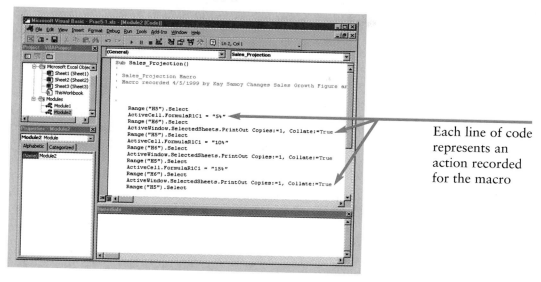

Each line of code
represents an
action recorded
for the macro

Excel 2000

Figure 5-6 Macro codes

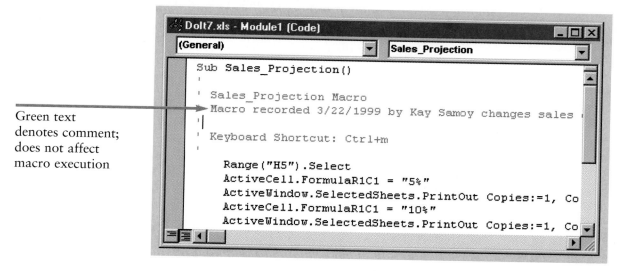

Green text
denotes comment;
does not affect
macro execution

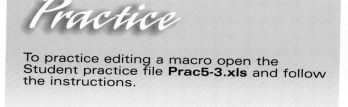

Practice

To practice editing a macro open the
Student practice file **Prac5-3.xls** and follow
the instructions.

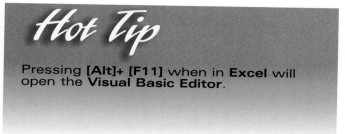

Hot Tip

Pressing **[Alt]+ [F11]** when in **Excel** will
open the **Visual Basic Editor**.

Adding a Macro to a Toolbar

Concept

A macro can be displayed as a button on a toolbar, using the Customize feature of the tools menu.

Do It!

Kay has decided that she wants to put a button on one of her toolbars that would activate the macro she has made.

1. Click Tools, then click Customize. The Customize dialog box appears.

2. Click the Commands tab to bring it to the front if it is not already there. The Categories area of this tab contains a list of menus, toolbars, and other locations where commands can be stored. The Commands section lists the commands that pertain to the selected category.

3. Scroll to the bottom of the Categories section and click Macros to select it. It will appear highlighted, as shown is **Figure 5-7**, to indicate its selection, and two custom commands appear in the Commands section.

4. Click the Custom button icon and drag it out of the dialog box and to the right end of the Standard toolbar. The mouse pointer will change to ▨ as it is dragged over the document window. The x in the box indicates that the button cannot be dropped there, but the pointer will be changed to ▨ when it is over a toolbar or menu. A short, vertical line I will appear on the toolbar indicating where the dropped button will be inserted. Place the button at the far right of the toolbar, after the Office Assistant button. The button appears where you inserted it, with a black border surrounding it to notify you that it is selected for modification, as shown in **Figure 5-8**.

5. Click ⌐Modify Selection ▾⌐ then click Assign Macro on the menu that appears. The Assign Macro dialog box opens, with the name of the macro you have made displayed.

6. Click the name of the macro, Sales_Projection, to make it appear in the Macro Name box. Then, click ⌐ OK ⌐. The button will now activate the selected macro when clicked.

Figure 5-7 Customize dialog box

Contains a list of all
Excel toolbars; check
items to make them
appear on the
Commands tab

List of Excel menus
and selected toolbars

Items displayed from
currently selected
toolbar or menu

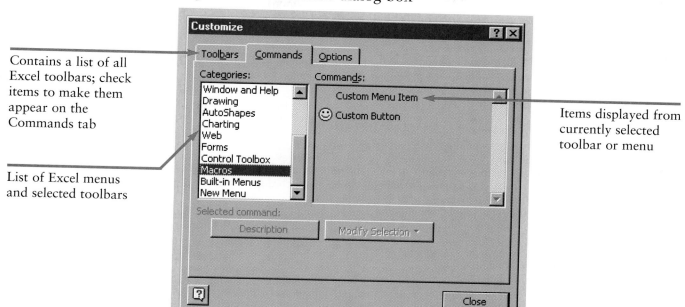

Excel 2000

Figure 5-8 Standard toolbar

Customized buttons,
borders indicate it is
selected for modification

EX 5.9

Adding a Macro to a Toolbar (continued)

Do It!

7 Click [Modify Selection ▾] , then triple click the Name text box near the top of the menu to select its contents.

8 Type Sales_Projection to name the button you have inserted. This will appear as the button's ScreenTip when you have finished.

9 Click Change Button Image on the Modify Selection menu, then click the calculator button ▦ on the palette of buttons that appears, as shown in **Figure 5-9**. The image on the button you inserted changes from a smiley face to a calculator.

10 Click [Close]. The dialog box closes, and the black border around the button disappears. The button is now active, and will run the designated macro if clicked. The toolbar on your screen should resemble the one in **Figure 5-10**.

11 Click the Sales_Projection button ▦ to run your macro. Notice that the value in Cell H5 is returned to 10% at the completion of the macro, reflecting the change you made in the previous skill.

12 Save your workbook.

More

When the Customize dialog box is open, buttons and menus can be selected and modified. Right-clicking a button or a command on a menu will bring up the Modify Command menu. The two Text Only commands let you control how a command appears. Selecting the Text Only (Always) command while the macro button is selected would make the button appear as [Sales_Projection] on a toolbar or menu. The Text Only (in Menus) command will make a menu command appear as text, without its assigned button icon next to it. The Image and Text command makes commands appear with both their names and their button icons whether they are located on a menu or toolbar.

Though Excel provides many icons to use on buttons that you create, you can also design your own. Click Edit Button Image on the Modify Command menu to bring up the Button Editor dialog box, shown in **Figure 5-11**. To change the color of one of the small squares (each one representing a single pixel), in the icon, just click it. The pixel will change to match the currently selected color. The Move section allows you to nudge the contents of the picture up, down, left or right, without having to redraw the entire image.

Figure 5-9 Palette of buttons

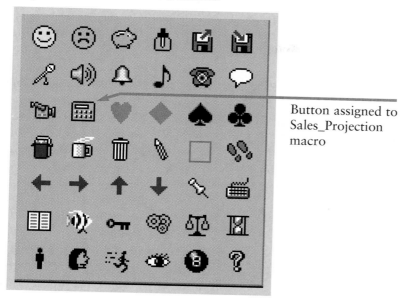

Button assigned to
Sales_Projection
macro

Figure 5-10 Standard toolbar with modified button

Figure 5-11 Button Editor box

Empty cells appear
transparent

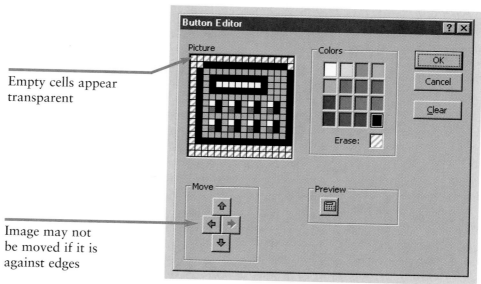

Image may not
be moved if it is
against edges

To practice adding a macro to a toolbar,
add the macro you created for
Practice5.xls to your toolbar.

Hot Tip

To remove a toolbar button or menu command, open the **Customize** dialog box and
drag the desired item from its toolbar or
menu to the dialog box.

Adding a Macro to a Menu

Concept

While having a macro on a toolbar is very helpful, you can also add to the functionality of the macro by adding it to a menu using the Customize feature of the Tools menu.

Do It!

Kay has decided that she wants to add a menu item that would activate the macro she has made.

1. Click Tools, then click Customize. The Customize dialog box appears.

2. Click the Commands tab to bring it to the front if it is not already there. The Categories area of this tab contains a list of menus, toolbars, and other locations where commands can be stored. The Commands section lists the commands that pertain to the selected category.

3. Scroll to the bottom of the Categories section and click Macros to select it. It will appear highlighted, as shown in **Figure 5-7** on page **EX 5.9**, to indicate its selection, and two custom commands appear in the Commands section.

4. Click the Custom menu item and drag it out of the dialog box and up to the Tools menu. The mouse pointer will change to ⬚ as it is dragged over the document window. The x in the box indicates that the button cannot be dropped there, but the pointer will be changed to ⬚ when it is over a menu. When the pointer is over a menu, the menu will open and a dark black horizontal line will appear on the menu indicating where the button will be inserted. Place the pointer over Macros in the menu, and wait for the submenu to open. When it does, place the pointer above the first submenu item, Macros..., and release the left mouse button. The command Custom menu item now appears at the top of the submenu.

5. Click **Modify Selection ▾** then click Assign Macro on the menu that appears. The Assign Macro dialog box opens, with the name of the macro you have made displayed.

6. Click the name of the macro, Sales_Projection, to make it appear in the Macro Name box, as shown in **Figure 5-12**. Then, click **OK**. The menu item will now activate the selected macro when clicked.

7. Click **Modify Selection ▾**, then triple-click the Name text box near the top of the menu to select its contents.

8. Type Run Sales_Projection to name the menu item you have inserted.

9. Click the Run Sales_Projection menu item to run your macro. Notice that the value in Cell H5 is returned to 10% at the completion of the macro, reflecting the change you made earlier.

10. Save your workbook.

More

You may customize any command which appears on any menu or toolbar, and you may also modify that button or commad. For example, if you don't want to click File every time you want to save a document as a Web page, you may put the command on a toolbar or in a menu which you access more often.

Figure 5-12 Assign Macro dialog box

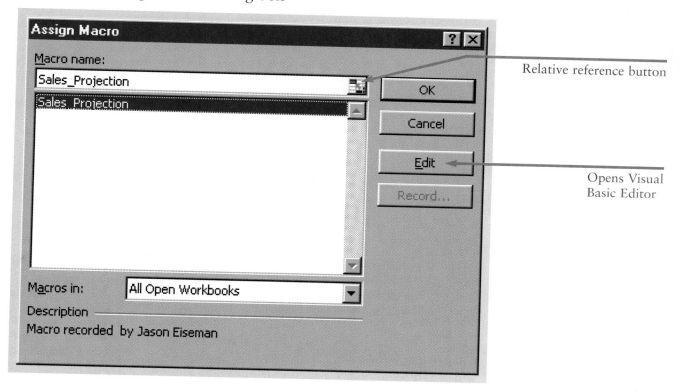

Relative reference button

Opens Visual
Basic Editor

Practice

To practice adding a macro to a menu, add the macro that you created in **Practice5.xls** to your **Tools** menu.

Hot Tip

Add an image to your menu by using the **Customize** menu. Select a menu item, select **Picture and Text**. Click **Select Button Image**, select an image. Open the menu, the picture you selected will appear in front of the menu command you created.

Copying Macros Across Files

Concept

Any macro that is created in one workbook can be used by other workbooks, provided the macro's original workbook is open. If there is a shortcut for a macro, such as a toolbar or menu command, and the parent file for the macro is not open, initiating the shortcut will cause Excel to open the macro's parent workbook before it applies the macro to the active workbook. Copying a macro from one workbook to another increases efficiency by allowing you to run the macro without having to open its parent file.

Do It!

Kay wants to copy her macro, Sales_Projection, from Profit2.xls to a workbook that contains her future business income and expenditures so that she can use it there.

1. Open Doit5-6.xls from your student disk. The workbook will be displayed in the window as the active document with Profit2 open behind it. The workbook is similar to Profit2.xls, but is for the following year's sales and expenses and lacks a chart or a macro.

2. Save Doit5-6.xls as Profit2000.xls in your student files. The workbook should now appear like the one shown in **Figure 5-13**.

3. Click Tools, highlight Macro, then select Visual Basic Editor from the submenu. **Figure 5-14** displays the Microsoft Visual Basic Window that will open.

4. The Project window in the Visual Basic Window displays the hierarchy of each of the open workbooks as icons labeled VBAProject (Profit2.xls) and VBA Project (Profit2000.xls) with their comments nested below. Click the ⊞ next to the upper icon. This will expand the hierarchy so you can view all the folders associated with that particular file. The Microsoft Excel Objects folder contains the worksheets for the workbook.

5. Click the ⊞ next to the Modules folder of Profit2.xls. The contents of the folder, Module, will be displayed, as shown in **Figure 5-15**. The Modules folder houses the macros for the workbook, and Module1 is the macro you created. Notice that the representation of Profit2000.xls does not show a modules folder since this file does not contain a macro.

Figure 5-13 Kay's worksheet for following year

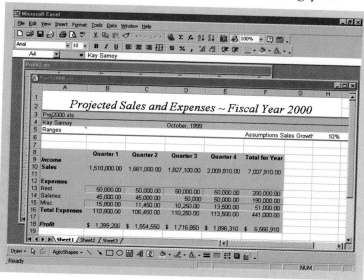

Figure 5-14 Visual Basic Editor

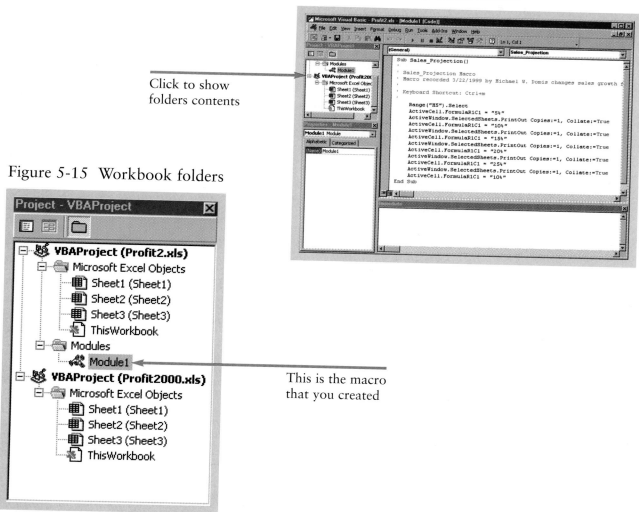

Click to show
folders contents

Figure 5-15 Workbook folders

This is the macro
that you created

Copying Macros Across Files (continued)

Do It!

6 Click and Drag Module1 onto the VBAProject (Profit2000.xls) icon, releasing the mouse button when the VBAProject (Profit 2000.xls) becomes highlighted see **Figure 5-16**. A new folder called Modules will appear in the VBAProject (Profit2000.xls) hierarchy, shown in **Figure 5-17**, containing the copied macro.

7 Click the Close button on the Visual Basic title bar to close the window.

8 Click Window, then click Profit2.xls to make it the active document window.

9 Close the file by clicking its Close button on the menu bar. The workbook will close, leaving Profit2.xls as the only open workbook.

10 Press [Ctrl]+[m] to run the macro. The macro will run as it did with Profit2.xls.

11 Close Profit2000.xls, saving changes when prompted to do so.

More

When you recorded the Sales_Projection macro it was saved only within the open workbook, Profit2.xls. This occurred because the default setting, This Workbook, was left unchanged in the Store Macro section of the Record Macro dialog box when you created the macro. In the above skill, you copied a macro to make it available to a workbook other than the macro's parent file. Copying is a good way to share case-specific macros, such as the Sales_Projection macro, between workbooks. However, if you create a macro that will be useful in many types of workbooks, such as one that inserts a custom header, copying it from workbook to workbook every time you want to use it would be tedious.

The Personal Macro Workbook lets you store macros so that they will be available to all Excel workbooks. You can save a macro directly into the Personal Macro Workbook by selecting Personal Macro Workbook in the Store macro in section of the Record Macro dialog box when you record the macro. This creates a workbook called Personal.xls in the Xlstart folder. A previously recorded macro can be copied to the Personal Macro Workbook in the same way that you copied macros between workbooks above. Once created, the Personal Macro Workbook will appear in the Visual Basic Project – VBAProject window just as any other workbook, and can be manipulated in the same manner. This workbook will be opened by Excel so as to make all of the macros it contains available to all open workbooks. Personal.xls is hidden by Excel so that it does not interfere with your work.

Figure 5-16 Copying a macro between workbooks

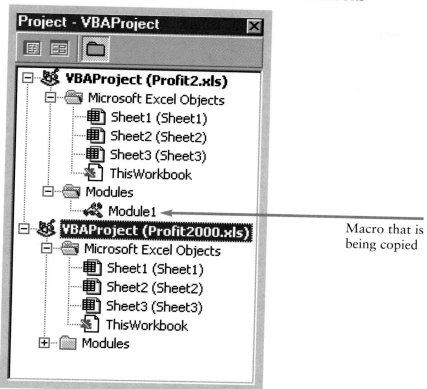

Macro that is
being copied

Figure 5-17 File hierarchy with copied macro

A new Modules folder is
automatically created to
house the copied macro

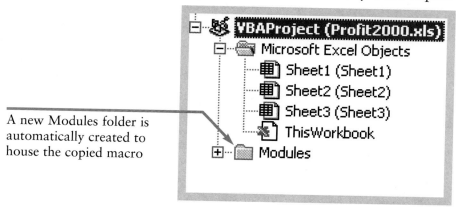

Practice

To practice copying a macro across workbooks, create a new workbook, save it as
MyPractice5-5.xls, then copy the
Expense_Report_Header macro to the new
workbook. Save both workbooks when
you are finished.

Hot Tip

When you create a toolbar button or menu
command for a macro, the shortcut
becomes linked to the parent work book of
the macro. If you use the toolbar button for
the Sales_Projection macro, Profit2.xls will
open if it is not already open.

Shortcuts

Function	Button/Mouse	Menu	Keyboard
Open Macro dialog box		Click Tools, then click Macro, then click Macros	[Alt]+[F8]
Open Visual Basic Editor		Click Tools, then click Macros, then click Visual Basic Editor	[Alt]+[F11]
Open Microsoft Script Editor		Click Tools, then click Macro, then Microsoft Script Editor	[Alt]+[Shift]+[F11]
Record New Macro		Click Tools, then click Macro, then click Record New Macro	
Stop Recording		Click Tools, then click Macro, then click Stop Recording	
Use Relative Cell References			
Interrupt a running macro			[Esc]

Identify Key Features

Name the items indicated by callouts in **Figure 5-18**.

Figure 5-18 Visual Basic Editor

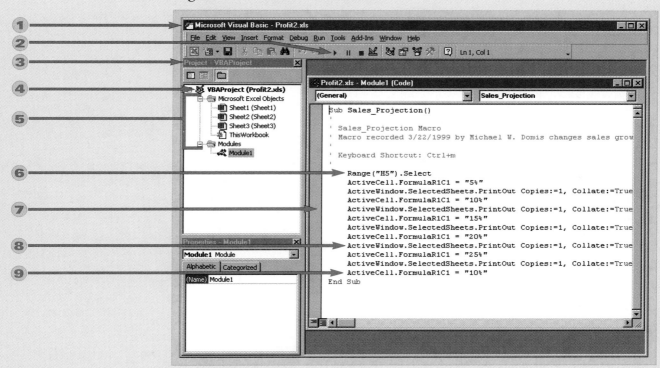

Select The Best Answer

10. A set of instructions that automates tasks you perform often.

11. Contains general commands for working with macros.

12. Allows you to make changes to a macro you have already recorded.

13. Opens Visual Basic in a debugging mode.

14. Click this to change the default way of referencing cells in a macro.

15. Use this command to customize tools.

16. This lets you store macros so that they will be available to all workbooks.

17. This allows you to change the appearance of a toolbar button.

18. This is the shortcut for opening the Visual Basic Editor.

19. Press this button when finished recording a macro.

a. Step Into button

b. Macro

c. Relative Reference button

d. Tools Menu

e. Visual Basic Editor

f. [Alt] + [F11]

g. Stop Recording button

h. Customize Command

i. Personal Macro Workbook

j. Button Editor Dialog box

Quiz (continued)

Complete the Statement

20. Using the Macro Option Dialog Box, you can edit:

    a. A macro's name

    b. A macro's name and description

    c. A macro's description and shortcut key

    d. A macro's name and shortcut key

21. To make a macro available to all workbooks, store it in the:

    a. My Documents folder

    b. Current Workbook

    c. All-Macro Workbook

    d. Personal Macro Workbook

22. You can determine all of the following in the Record Macro dialog box except:

    a. Macro's name

    b. Macro's steps

    c. Place the macro will be stored

    d. Macro's shortcut key

23. The Relative Reference button is located on the:

    a. Stop Recording toolbar

    b. Macro toolbar

    c. Record toolbar

    d. Visual Basic Editor

24. To add a macro to a toolbar, access the Customize Dialog box from the:

    a. Macro dialog box

    b. Option dialog box

    c. Tools menu

    d. Options menu

25. If you use a shortcut to a macro that has not been copied to the current workbook, Excel will:

    a. Run the macro

    b. Create a parent workbook for the macro

    c. Delete the shortcut

    d. Open the macro's parent workbook

26. Pressing [Alt] + [F8] will:

    a. Open the Visual Basic Editor

    b. Run a macro

    c. Open Macro Dialog box

    d. Interrupt a running macro

27. The name that you give a new toolbar button will also appear as its:

    a. Shortcut key

    b. ScreenTip

    c. Macro

    d. Menu item

28. The default setting for storing a macro is:

    a. That workbook

    b. This workbook

    c. Those workbooks

    d. Which workbooks

29. Each of the small squares in the Button Editor dialog box represents a single:

    a. Date

    b. Command

    c. Pixel

    d. Fairy

Interactivity

Test Your Skills

1. Record a macro that will calculate the average time you spend doing an activity over the five days of the work week:

   a. Open the file Test 4.xls which you created at the end of the previous Lesson.

   b. Place a label that reads Five Day Average directly to the right of the Average label.

   c. Select the cell where the Five Day Average column intersects with the Class row.

   d. Open the Record Macro dialog box. Name the macro Five_Day_Average, make the Shortcut key [Ctrl]+[m], and add a second line to the description that reads Calculates average for Monday thru Friday.

   e. When you click OK in the Macro dialog box, the Stop Recording toolbar should appear. If not, activate it from the View menu.

   f. Begin recording the macro; click the Relative Reference button; click the Paste Function button; select the Average function; when the Average dialog box asks for Number 1, collapse the dialog box; select the cells that contain the Class data for Monday through Friday; expand the dialog box and click OK; click the Stop Recording button.

   g. When you stopped recording the macro, the average time you spend in class Monday through Friday should have appeared in the Class row of the Five Day Average column.

2. Run a macro:

   a. Select the cell in the Activities row of the Five Day Average column.

   b Open the Macro dialog box.

   c. Run the Five_Day_Average macro to calculate the time you spend participating in activities Monday through Friday.

   d. Select the cell in the Meals row of the Five Day Average column.

   e. Run the Five_Day_Average macro using its shortcut key.

   f. Use the macro you created to calculate the five day averages for the remaining daily activities.

3. View the code for the macro you created:

   a. Open the Visual Basic Editor.

   b. Select Module 1 in the Project window, and look over its code (if the code is not visible, click the View Code button).

   c. Close Microsoft Visual Basic

4. Add a button for the Five_Day_Average macro to the Standard toolbar and save the workbook as Test 5.xls.

Interactivity (continued)

Test Your Skills

5. Change the image of the toolbar button you created from the smiley face to the key.

6. Place the macro you created on the menu bar, using the customize command.

7. Change the macro name to Run Sales_Projection.

Problem Solving

Oliver's bakery is a newly opened take-out store in your town that features a variety of bagels, fresh breads, croissants, cookies, and coffee. Demand for freshly prepared take-out food is high, so business is booming. The owner of Oliver's, Oliver Rhodes, has already had to hire six employees. Oliver currently processes the payroll manually. He makes all of the calculations for salary, deductions, and net pay using a hand-held calculator. Then he types the results onto a Payroll Register sheet. A Payroll Register is a report prepared for each payroll period that lists the names, gross pay, deductions, and net pay for each employee, and the total gross pay, deductions, and net pay for that payroll period.

Oliver would like to use his time more effectively to promote his business and to develop new varieties of baked goods and coffee. He also wants to curb the danger of making miscalculations in the payroll. Oliver feels that since there are relatively few checks to write, this part of the process can remain manual. However, he could save many hours if all of the payroll calculations and the preparation of the Payroll Register report could be animated.

It is your job to develop a worksheet that creates a Payroll Register report for Oliver's. The basic format of the Payroll Register includes the pay period, the names of the employees, social security numbers, hours worked, and hourly pay rate. The worksheet should automatically calculate weekly gross pay, net pay, and all deductions for each employee. It should also provide totals for each of these categories for the pay period. Weekly gross pay can be calculated by multiplying pay rate by hours worked. Net pay is gross pay minus all deductions. Use the following figures to calculate deductions: Federal withholding tax=9.25 % of gross pay; State withholding tax=2.5% of gross pay; Social Security (FICA)=6.2% of gross pay; Medicare=1.45% of gross pay. Enter theses figures as assumptions in your worksheet.

It is up to you to create the hours worked and pay rate data, so use realistic figures. When constructing the worksheet, be sure to take advantage of Excel's most useful features such as formatting, cell referencing, formulas, and macros. The Payroll Register report should fit on one page when you print it. When you have finished, save the file to your student disk as Solved 5.xls.

L E S S O N

EXPLORING FORMULAS AND FUNCTIONS

E ach Excel 2000 worksheet can contain over 16 million cells. Using these cells, you can create formulas to calculate payments, statistics, and time parameters.

With that many possible cells, however, the process of creating formulas can be daunting. While it is possible to create a formula by naming each individual cell to be included in the formula, Excel allows us a faster, more convenient way.

By using Range Names you can simplify the formula process. Ranges are a defined series of cells. This series can include adjacent or nonadjacent cells. Once you have selected cells that contain similar information, you can name the range and thus use the name to calculate.

In this chapter, you will learn about naming ranges, and how to use those range names in certain formulas. For example, using a Range Name, you can calculate a monthly payment amount, or calculate statistics for your spreadsheet. Excel also offers you the opportunity to create formulas using dates to calculate when invoices are due. Or, using conditional formulas, when payments on those invoices are overdue.

In sum, by using Range Names and formulas you can perform calculations on your spreadsheets that used to be the domain of accountants.

Case Study:
Kay will use many of the functions available in Excel to perform calculations which are useful when you are using workbooks for financial organization. She will use different formulas and functions, as well as performing multiple calculations to perform complex tasks.

Creating Formulas with Range Names

Concept

One way of creating formulas is to name each individual cell that will be used in the formula. However, Excel offers an easier way for creating formulas by using the Range names in place of the actual cell names. Range names are usually easier to remember than cell names and ranges cover a broader territory than individual cells.

Do It!

Kay will calculate the total of her expenses for each quarter of the year by creating a formula with range names instead of cell numbers.

1 Open Student File Doit6-1.xls.

2 Click on cell B13 and drag down to Cell B15 to select those three cells.

3 In the Name Box, these cells are now listed as B13 (see **Figure 6-1**).

4 Click the Name Box to highlight it.

5 Type Q1_Expenses. Don't forget the underline ([Shift]+[-]), as range labels cannot have spaces.

6 Hit [Enter] to accept the Range name.

7 Double-click Cell A19 to type in it. Type Total in the cell.

8 Click cell B19 once to select it.

9 Click once in the formula bar.

10 Type the following formula,=Sum(Q1_Expenses).

11 Press Enter.

12 The total of Q1_Expenses is now entered in cell B19. Your worksheet should now look like **Figure 6-2**.

More

Remember, you can name a range using any number of adjacent or nonadjacent cells. This means that ranges can consists of entire columns, or parts of columns; Entire rows, or parts of rows; and all the cells in the table, or only selected cells in the table. It is up to you as to what cells you want to include in a range.

Any time you add text to a worksheet you should be sure to check the spelling. When you finish designing a worksheet you ashould also be sure to check the spelling. To do this click Tools, then click Spelling, or click the Spelling button on the Standard toolbar, to start the Spell Checker.

Figure 6-1 Worksheet with range selected

Range name

Range is
selected

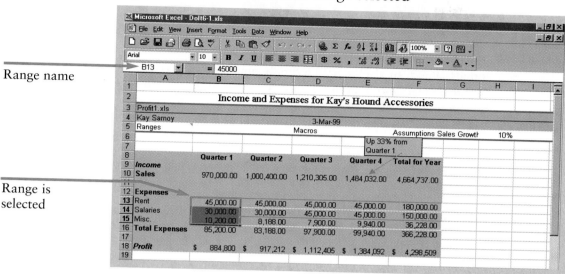

Excel 2000

Figure 6-2 Worksheet with a named range

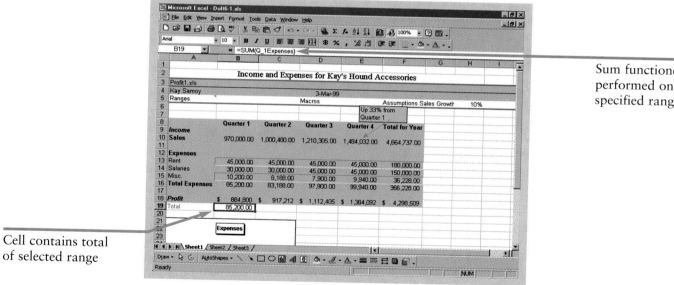

Sum functioned
performed on
specified range

Cell contains total
of selected range

Practice

To practice using Range names in formulas,
Save the chart on the screen as
Profit999.xls, and then create and total the
ranges for the second, third and fourth
quarters.

Hot Tip

You can select nonadjacent cells for a
range by holding down the **[shift]** key, and
then clicking on as many cells as you want
in the range.

Applying a Function to Multiple Ranges

Concept

Range names can also be used to apply functions such as the Sum Function, or the Average Function to a group of cells. In addition, Excel allows you to add a function to multiple ranges, thus allowing you to easily calculate averages using Range names instead of having to type all the cells into the function.

Do It!

Kay is going to average her quarterly expenses for the first six months using the Average function and Range names.

1. Open Student file Doit6-2.xls.

2. Double-click on cell A20. Type Averages in the cell.

3. Click on cell C20 to select it.

4. Click on the ▣ in the formula bar. The Edit Formula box will open with the Equal sign already in place.

5. Click the drop-down arrow in the Formula Palette to open the list of available functions (currently, the Formula Palette has the word Average in it).

6. Click on Average to select it.

7. Now, the formula in the formula bar reads =Average(C18:C19) as seen in **Figure 6-3**. The function is correct, but the cells are wrong.

8. To correct this, move the insertion bar until it is in front of the first C in C18, and click once.

9. Press Delete seven times to erase the argument.

10. Now, type Q1_Expenses:Q2_Expenses inside the parentheses.

11. Press Enter to run the function.

12. Cell C20 now reads 28,064.67, which is the average expense for the first two quarters (see **Figure 6-4**).

More

Excel has many different ways of providing help to you. If, for example, you incorrectly enter a formula into the formula bar, when you press [Enter] to calculate, Excel will show a message box. The message box will say that the formula is entered incorrectly and ask if you would like Excel to enter the correct formula.

Figure 6-3 Worksheet with specified ranges

Formula Palette

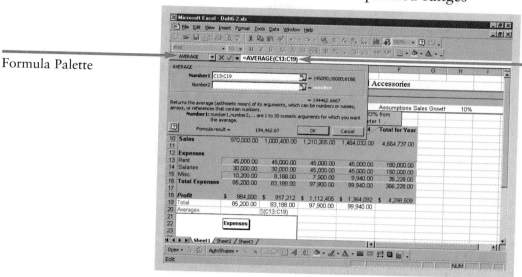

Specifies function
to be performed
on cell range

Figure 6-4 Worksheet displaying range averages

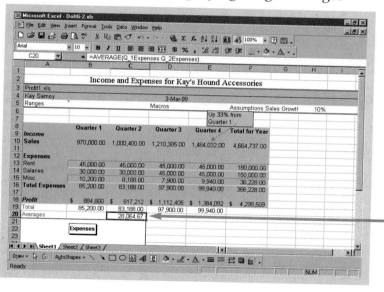

Displays the average for
multiple cell ranges

Practice

Using the Range names for all four
quarters, calculate the average expense for
the year.

Hot Tip

While typing a formula, you can also click
on the range using the mouse to enter it
into the formula, rather than typing out its
name.

Calculating with Dates

Concept

By entering dates in a worksheet so that Excel recognizes them as dates, you can sort the dates and perform date calculations. Date calculations are helpful when a company issues invoices.

Do It!

Kay will calculate the invoice due dates for her open invoices, as well as the age of the invoices.

1. From your student files, open Doit6-3.xls.

2. Click on the sheet 2 tab at the bottom of the worksheet to access Kay's Hound Accessories Accounts Receivable Worksheet (see **Figure 6-5**).

3. Click on cell F9 to activate it and place the insertion bar in it.

4. Type an Equals sign [=].

5. Click on cell B9 to add it to the formula.

6. Type a plus sign [+], then the number 30 to complete the formula.

7. Press [Enter]. The date in cell F9 (see **Figure 6-6**) is now the original invoice date plus 30 days.

8. To apply the formula to the rest of the invoices, make sure cell F9 is the active cell, and then click and drag the fill bar down to cell F15. Release the mouse button.

9. Excel applies the formula to all the cells you selected using the Random Cell Reference feature. Your sheet should now look like the one in **Figure 6-7**.

Figure 6-5 Accounts Receivable worksheet

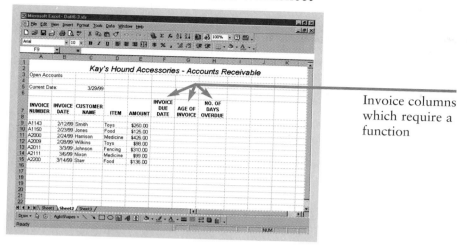

Invoice columns
which require a
function

Figure 6-6 Worksheet with original invoice date

The original
invoice date
plus 30 days

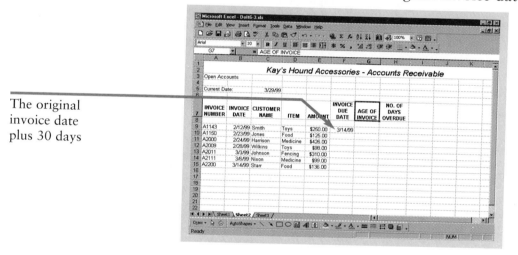

Figure 6-7 Worksheet after formula is applied

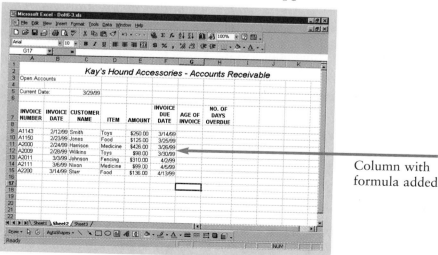

Column with
formula added

Calculating with Dates (continued)

Do It

10 To calculate the age of the invoice, click on cell G9 to activate it.

11 Type an Equals sign [=].

12 Click on cell C5 to add it to the formula.

13 Press the F4 key to make it the Absolute Cell reference. By doing this, all the cells that use this formula will refer to C5 for the calculation.

14 Type a minus sign [-].

15 Click on Cell B9 to add it to the formula. The completed formula should look like **Figure 6-8**.

16 Press [Enter] to calculate the formula.

17 Notice that Excel shows you another date. This means you must change formats.

18 Click on Cell G9, and then click on Format on the toolbar.

19 Click on Cells... from the format menu.

20 Bring the Number tab to the front, and select the General category (see **Figure 6-9**). Click [OK].

21 Now, you have the correct age of the invoice, which is 41 days, in cell G9.

22 To transfer the formula to the other cells, click and drag the fill handle of cell G9 down to cell G15. The age of each invoice is now displayed in days. Your sheet should now look like **Figure 6-10**.

More

When you enter a date in Excel, and want to use the date to do calculations, you must remember to enter dates so that Excel recognizes them as dates. The most common way of entering a date is mm/dd/yy, or 3/3/99. Another common way is mmm/dd/yyyy, or Mar 3, 1999. Either of these ways is acceptable to Excel, as it will automatically change the date into a format it can work with.

Figure 6-8 Formula bar

Absolute cell reference

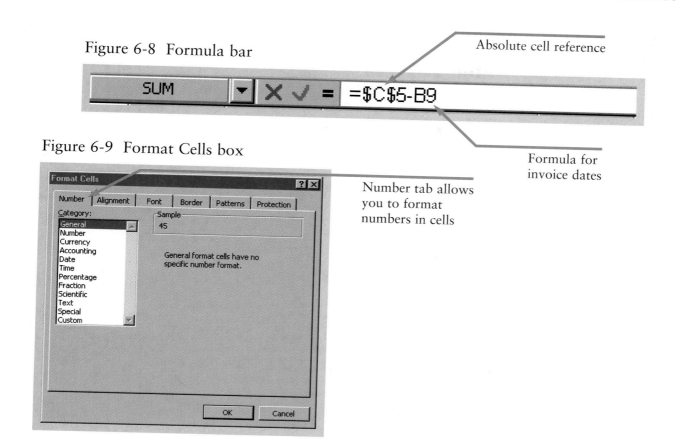

SUM ▼ X ✓ = =$C$5-B9

Formula for
invoice dates

Figure 6-9 Format Cells box

Number tab allows
you to format
numbers in cells

Figure 6-10 Worksheet with invoice age

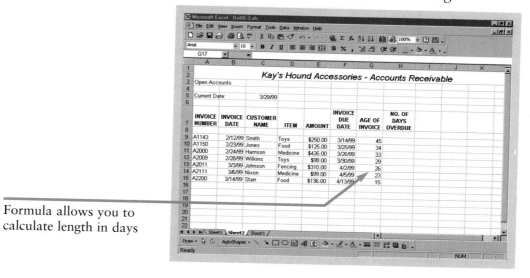

Formula allows you to
calculate length in days

Practice

For more practice calculating with dates,
open the Student practice File **Prac6-3.xls**.
Save it as **MyPractice6**, and then follow
the instructions on the **Prac6-3** worksheet.

Hot Tip

You can perform time calculations in Excel.
Enter the starting and ending times and
Excel will calculate how many hours and
minutes something took. You must enter
the time in a format that Excel recognizes:
For example, 2:15 PM (hh:mm AM/PM).

Using Conditional Formulas

Concept

A conditional formula is one where specific criteria have to be met before the formula will finish calculating. If the criteria of the formula are not met, Excel will tell you so.

Do It!

Kay will set up a conditional formula to calculate if any of her invoices are overdue.

1 Open Student File Doit6-4.xls, and click on sheet 2 tab to bring it to the front.

2 Click on cell H9.

3 Click on the Equal sign ▣ in the formula bar to activate the Edit Formula dialog box.

4 Click on the drop-down arrow in the formula selection box, and select the IF function.

5 The Create Formula dialog box opens with three text boxes (see **Figure 6-11**). The first text box is the Logical_test text box. Type G9>30 in the first text box. This tells the program to check if the number in cell G9 is greater than (>) 30.

6 Click on the middle text box to select it. This is the Value if True text box. The formula entered here tells the program what to do if the logical test is true. Type G9-30 in this box. So, if the test is true, Excel will then subtract 30 from the number in cell G9, and enter the result.

7 Click the bottom text box. This is the Value if False text box. What is entered here tells the program how to respond if the first part of the formula is false. Type 0 (zero) here.

8 Your formula box should now look like **Figure 6-12**. Click [OK] to run the formula.

9 The result in cell H9 now reads 11.

10 Click on cell H9 to activate the fill handle. Click and drag the fill bar over cells H10 through H15. Release the mouse button, and Excel will apply the formula in H9 to the selected cells and return the correct result, using the random cell reference feature.

More

While conditional formulas might seem confusing, there is an easier way to view them. All conditional formulas have three parts. The first part of the formula tells the program to verify something. The second part of the formula tells the program what to do if the first part is true. The third part of the formula tells the computer what to do if the first part is false.

Figure 6-11 Create Formula dialog box

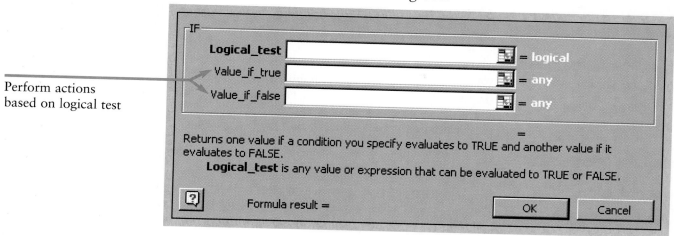

Perform actions
based on logical test

Figure 6-12 Conditional formula

Displays the result of the formula
based on the logical test and the
True or False value

Practice

For more practice using conditional
formulas, open the student practice file
Prac6-4.xls and follow the instructions.

Hot Tip

You must enter a value in the **Value if
False** text box of the **Edit Formula** dialog
box. Failure to enter a numerical value will
result in the program using the word **False**
to show that the condition was not met.

Using Statistical Functions

Concept

While Excel may offer several hundred worksheet functions, there are only six statistical functions that it offers. These functions allow you to calculate an average, count the number of nonblank entries, count the number of values, calculate a total, find the smallest value, or find the largest value.

Do It!

Although Kay only has seven invoices now, she wants to create statistics to track her invoices. Specifically, she will create statistics concerning the oldest invoice, the newest invoice, and the total number of invoices.

1. Click on cell A17 to activate it, and type Statistics for Invoices.

2. Click on cell A18, and type Total Number of Invoices:.

3. Click on cell A19 and type Newest Invoice:.

4. Click on cell A20 and type Oldest Invoice:. Check your worksheet against **Figure 6-13** for accuracy.

5. Click on cell D18. This is where you will calculate the total number of invoices.

6. Type an Equal sign [=] followed by the word Counta.

7. Type an Open parenthesis [(], and the range G9:G15. Type a Close parenthesis [)].

8. Check your formula against **Figure 6-14** and then press [Enter].

9. The number 7 is now displayed in cell D18. This is the total number of invoices.

10. Click on cell D19 to begin calculating the newest invoice.

11. Type an Equal [=] sign, then MIN. Type an Open parenthesis [(] followed by the range G9:G15. Type a Close parenthesis [)]. Check your work against and press [Enter].

Figure 6-13 Worksheet with statistical categories

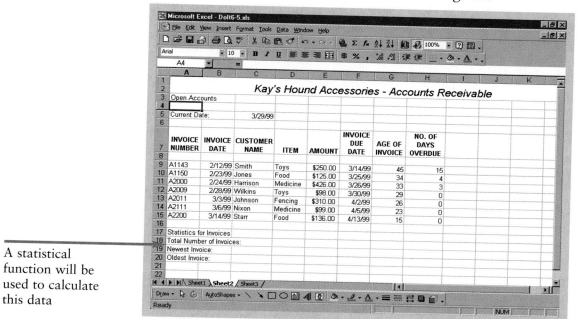

A statistical
function will be
used to calculate
this data

Excel 2000

Statistical function
for calculating
invoice data

Figure 6-14 Formula bar

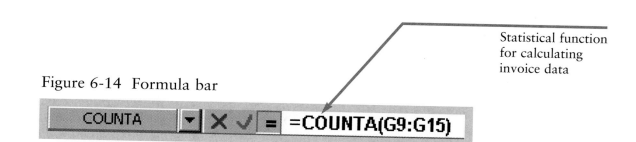

Using Statistical Functions (continued)

Do It!

12 In cell D19 the number 15 represents the age in days of the newest invoice.

13 Click Cell D20 to enter the formula to find the oldest invoice .otr Ho

14 Type an Equal [=] sign, followed by Max' and then an Open Parenthesis [(].

15 Type the range G9:G15, and a close parenthesis [)]. Check your formula against **Figure 6-15** and then press [Enter].

16 The result displayed in cell D20 is the age of the oldest invoice. Your sheet should now match **Figure 6-16**. Save your work.

More

Instead of typing the function name into the formula, you can use the Paste Formula function. By selecting a cell, and then clicking on ▣ in the formula bar, you will see a small drop-down arrow appear next to the formula name and the Edit formula box will open. By clicking on the drop-down arrow, you can access the more common functions of Excel. By clicking on a function, you paste it into the formula window so that all you have to do is add the range.

Figure 6-15 Statistical function

MAX ▼ ✕ ✓ = **=MAX(G9:G15)** ←────────── Function to
be performed

Figure 6-16 Worksheet with statistical functions

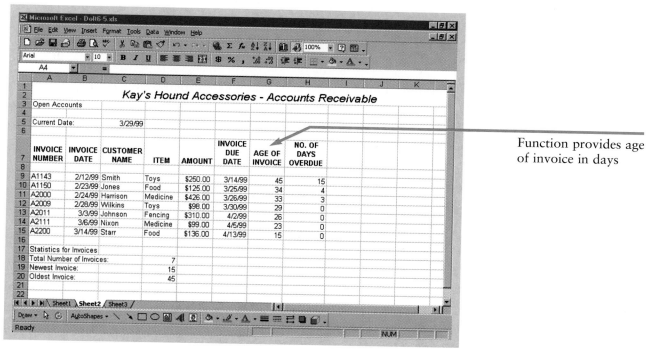

Function provides age
of invoice in days

Using the PMT Function to Calculate Payments

Concept

PMT is a financial function that will calculate the periodic payment amount for money borrowed. It also allows companies to loan money to customers and calculate the appropriate repayment amounts.

Do It!

Kay has issued credit cards to her best customers. She now needs to calculate the repayment amounts for these customers based on 12% simple interest and a variable term dependant on the amount the customer charged.

1 Open student file Doit6-6.xls. Using the sheet tabs, bring the third sheet to the front (see **Figure 6-17**).

2 Click cell F6 to activate it.

3 Click ▣ on the formula bar to activate the drop-down list.

4 Open the drop-down list and click more functions. The Paste Function dialog box will open (see **Figure 6-18**).

5 Click the Financial function category.

6 From the Function name list, click on PMT. Click ▭OK▭ .

7 The PMT dialog box is now open (see **Figure 6-19**). You should move it so that you can see the table.

8 The first number, Rate, is the interest rate, and the period the interest is charged. Type .12/12 here.

9 Place the insertion bar in the Nper text box and click once. Nper is the total number of payments for the loan. Click on Cell E6 to enter the total number of payments.

10 Place the insertion bar in the Pv text box and click once. Pv is the Present value of the loan. Click cell C6 to select it as the Pv.

Figure 6-17 Sheet 3 in workbook

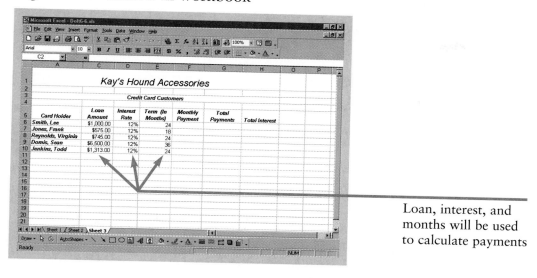

Loan, interest, and
months will be used
to calculate payments

Excel 2000

Figure 6-18 Paste Function dialog box

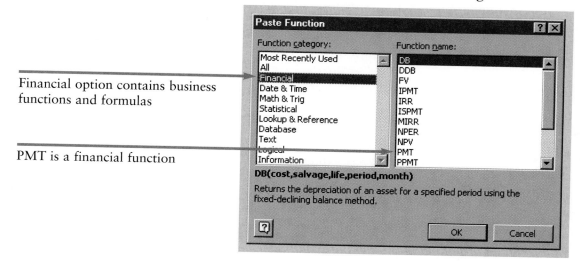

Financial option contains business
functions and formulas

PMT is a financial function

Figure 6-19 PMT dialog box

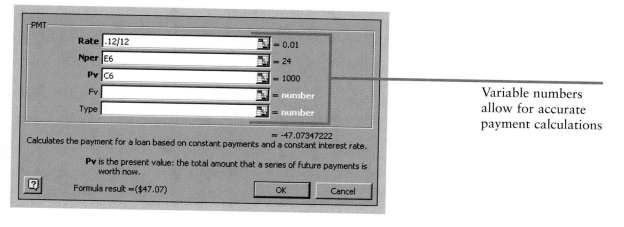

Variable numbers
allow for accurate
payment calculations

Using the PMT Function to Calculate Payments (continued)

Do It!

11 Check your work against **Figure 6-20** and then click [OK] to have Excel calculate the payment.

12 Notice that the payment has a minus sign in front of it, or is in red with parentheses around it. This indicates a negative number. To change this to a positive number, place the insertion bar in front of the C in C6 on the formula bar and click once. Type a minus sign [-]. Press [Enter]. The amount is now a positive, showing how much the customer must pay per month.

13 Click cell F6 to activate it. Click and drag the fill handle down to highlight cells F7, F8, F9, and F10. Release the mouse.

14 Using the Random Cell reference feature, Excel now calculates the monthly payments for the other credit card customers (see **Figure 6-21**).

15 Save the worksheet.

More

It is important to be consistent about the rates you use for Nper and Rate. If you choose to express Nper as the number of monthly payments, then you must express the interest rate as Percentage/months, or .12/12, indicating 12% interest for 12 months.

Figure 6-20 PMT dialog box with formulas added

Interest rate over
period of months

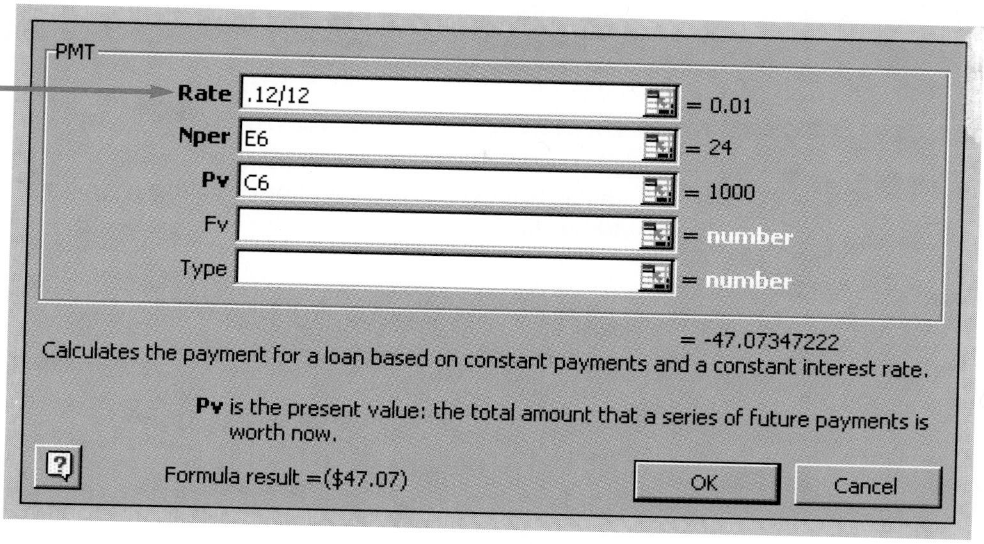

PMT			
Rate	.12/12		= 0.01
Nper	E6		= 24
Pv	C6		= 1000
Fv			= number
Type			= number

= -47.07347222

Calculates the payment for a loan based on constant payments and a constant interest rate.

Pv is the present value: the total amount that a series of future payments is worth now.

Formula result =($47.07)   [OK]   [Cancel]

Excel 2000

Figure 6-21 Monthly payments for credit card customers

		Credit Card Customers		
Card Holder	Loan Amount	Interest Rate	Term (In Months)	Monthly Payment
Smith, Lee	$1,000.00	12%	24	$47.07
Jones, Frank	$575.00	12%	18	$35.06
Reynolds, Virginia	$745.00	12%	24	$35.07
Domis, Sean	$6,500.00	12%	36	$215.89
Jenkins, Todd	$1,313.00	12%	24	$61.81

Monthly payments are
calculated by specified
months and interest rate

Practice

For additional practice with payments, open student practice file **Prac6-6.xls** and follow the instructions.

Hot Tip

You can enter a formula by typing in the appropriate values in the formula bar. However, if you use values instead of cell references, you cannot use the fill handle option to click and drag the formula to other cells.

Displaying and Printing Formulas

Concept

Most of the time, Excel will use the formulas that you enter, but will hide those formulas from view. You can, however, display and print the formulas to check them for accuracy.

Do It!

Kay has used a number of formulas in her tables, and she wishes to display and print them to make sure they are correct.

1. With sheet 3 of the student file Doit6-6.xls on the screen, click on Tools in the menu bar.

2. Click Options from the Tools menu. The Options dialog box will open (see **Figure 6-22**).

3. Click the View tab to bring it to the front.

4. In the Windows options, click the Formulas check box to select it.

5. Click ⬛ OK ⬛ in the Options dialog box.

6. Scroll slowly to the right on your worksheet to bring all the formulas into view. Your sheet should resemble **Figure 6-23**.

7. Click the Print Preview button on the Standard toolbar.

8. Notice that the formulas are not shown in the portrait orientation. Click the Landscape option radio button.

9. Now that you can see all of the formulas, click the Print button in the Print Preview window, then click ⬛ OK ⬛.

10. Your worksheet is now sent to the printer showing the formulas you used on the sheet. To return to the regular view and see the results of the formulas only, press [Ctrl]+[`].

More

There are a number of other options you can select in the Print Preview mode. For instance, by clicking the Fit to option, you can instruct the machine to fit all the information on a single page for printing. You can also experiment with different settings in the Print Preview mode before printing to get the look you want for your worksheet.

Figure 6-22 Options dialog box

Controls the way the worksheet is displayed on the screen

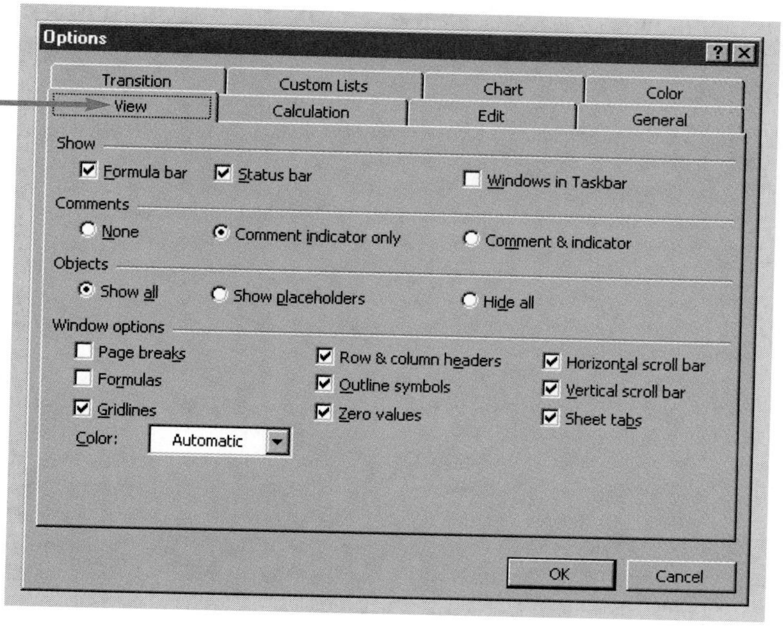

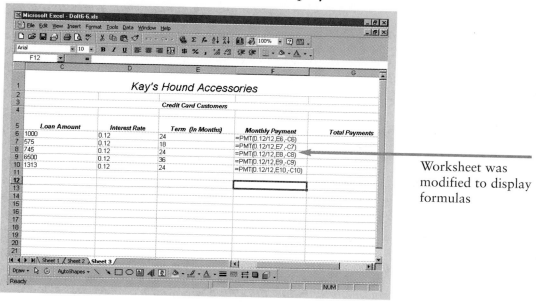

Figure 6-23 Worksheet with formulas displayed

Worksheet was modified to display formulas

Excel 2000

Practice

For more practice displaying and printing formula, click the Print Preview button on your screen, and choose different settings to see what effect they have on your worksheet.

Hot Tip

All page setup options, such as portrait orientation, fit to scaling, and printing row and column headings, apply to the active worksheet only, and are saved with the workbook.

Shortcuts

Function	Button/Mouse	Menu	Keyboard
Opens Formula Palette, displays function results	=		
Paste function	fx	Click Insert, then click Function	
Format Cells	🏠	Click Format, then click Cells	[Ctrl]+[1]
AutoSum	Σ		
Currency style	$		
Refresh all data	🔄		

Identify Key Features

Name the items indicated by callouts in **Figure 6-24**.

Figure 6-24   Excel Worksheet

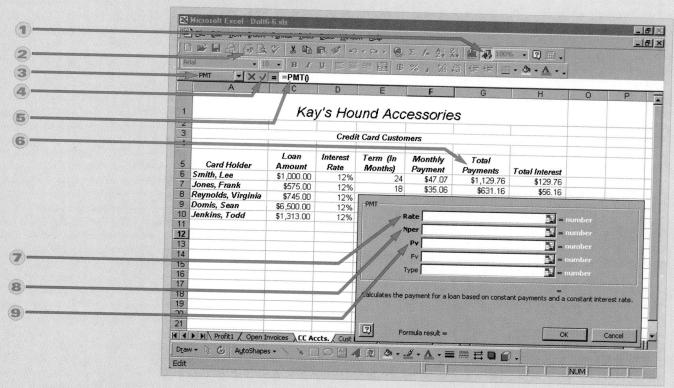

Select The Best Answer

10. The small square in the lower-right corner of the active cell.

11. The function used to calculate payments.

12. One way to enter a date.

13. This symbol [>] means.

14. Calculates an average value.

15. This must be at the beginning of any conditional formula.

16. This statistical function returns the largest in a set of values.

17. This button on the toolbar allows you to see how your document will print.

a. PMT

b. Greater than

c. Print Preview Button

d. 1/1/00

e. IF

f. MAX

g. Average

h. Fill handle

Quiz (continued)

Complete the Statement

18. When naming a range, it's important to remember that it cannot have any:

    a. Numbers in it

    b. Spaces in it

    c. More than 5 alphanumeric characters

    d. Letters in it

19. Ranges can be made up of:

    a. Rows

    b. Columns

    c. Non-adjacent cells

    d. All of the above

20. An incorrect way of entering dates would be:

    a. 3/3/99

    b. Mar 3, 1999

    c. 1999, March 3

    d. March 3, 1999

21. The statistical function to find the total number of items in a worksheet is:

    a. Min

    b. Counta

    c. Max

    d. Average

22. The function to calculate the period payment amount is:

    a. PMT

    b. PV

    c. Nper

    d. Per

23. Nper is:

    a. The rate of the loan

    b. The time period of the loan

    c. The value of the loan

    d. The total number of payments for the loan

24. There are two ways to orient a worksheet for printing. Landscape is one way, the other way is:

    a. Vertical

    b. Portrait

    c. Horizontal

    d. Picture

25. A conditional formula has three parts. One of them is NOT:

    a. The Logical test

    b. The Value if True

    c. The Value if False

    d. The Logical value

Interactivity

Test Your Skills

1. Choose the Sum formula from the formula selection box:
   a. Click on the Equal sign in the formula bar.
   b. Click on the drop-down arrow.
   c. Scroll down and click on Sum in the list.
   d. Name a range:
   e. Using click and drag, select four cells.
   f. Click the name box.
   g. Type a name for the range.
   h. Press Enter.

2. Calculate the average amount of Kay's credit cards:
   a. Type **Average Owed:** in cell A12 of worksheet 3.
   b. Click cell B12 to activate it.
   c. Click on the Equal sign in the formula bar.
   d. Select Average from the drop-down list.
   e. Click inside the parentheses to select them.
   f. Type B6:B10.
   g. Press Enter.

3. Preview and Print the worksheet:
   a. Switch to Print Preview mode.
   b. Zoom in on the right side of the worksheet.
   c. Change the orientation of the page landscape.
   d. Print the worksheet.
   e. Return to Normal view.

Excel 2000

Interactivity (continued)

Problem Solving

Using your skills, create an additional statistic for worksheet 2 calculating the average amount of all the invoices.

Create a new column for worksheet two titled Days until Due. Create a conditional formula to calculate how many days until each invoice is due.

For worksheet 3, create a new row titled Monthly Amount Incoming. Calculate the total amount of credit card payments that Kay can expect.

Kay gives Jeb Magruder a credit card. He promptly charges $215.00. Add his name to worksheet 3, and calculate his monthly payment based on a rate of 10% for 18 months. (Hint: Check the formula. Don't trust the program on this one.)

Kay has four customers for whom she does dog grooming. Create a worksheet for these customers and calculate the amount each would owe if Kay groomed their dogs for the following times and charged the following amounts.

Customer A: 8 AM to 9:15 AM; $6 an hour.

Customer B: 9:30 AM to 10:45 AM; $5.50 an hour.

Customer C: 11 AM to 12:15 PM; $6.50 an hour.

Customer D: 1:15 PM to 2:45 PM; $5.00 an hour.

L E S S O N

MANAGING YOUR WORKBOOKS

As you've seen in previous lessons, Excel has the ability to create and store tremendous amounts of information in spreadsheets. As a matter of fact, a single spreadsheet can have over 16 million cells of information. And, each workbook can contain over a hundred worksheets. Keeping track of all this data can be a daunting task, especially when, at times, you want to print or view only specific data.

The makers of Excel understand this, and have given you several management functions within the program. Using these functions, you will be able to change the way you view data. You will also be able to print just the data you need. And, you will be able to secure your data so that no one can alter it. Using the data management functions in Excel, you can Freeze Panes in a window, insert and delete worksheets, create custom views, hide data and formulas, insert page breaks, and adjust the setup of pages.

When you learn to manage your workbooks, you will also find that you can reference one worksheet with another and thereby increase Excel's capabilities.

Case Study:
In this lesson, Kay will use Excel's workbook management techniques to change the way she views data, and to print reports utilizing these views. She will also secure her worksheet and reference two sheets within the workbook.

Using the Freeze Panes Command

Concept

Consider the fact that an Excel worksheet can contain 256 columns. Consider also that the same worksheet can contain 65,533 rows. Realize that this means there are a possible 16,776,448 cells of information. Try to imagine scrolling through 15,550,352 cells to get to the data you need. While you're imagining this time-consuming task, you might also consider that there is an easier way. Excel allows you to temporarily freeze columns and rows. These frozen areas are called panes and can minimize the time you spend looking for data in a large worksheet.

Do It!

Kay is going to freeze a column on her invoice worksheet so that she can quickly check on the number of days until the invoice is due.

1. Open the Student workbook titled Doit7-1.xls and click the Open Accounts tab to bring it to the front.

2. Click on cell D6 to make it the active cell.

3. Click on Window in the menu bar.

4. Click on the Freeze Window command. Everything to the left and above the active cell will be frozen. This is indicated by the two dark intersecting lines (see **Figure 7-1**).

5. To bring the correct data into alignment, click five times on the right pointing, horizontal scroll button.

6. The data is now aligned correctly. You can easily see the customer name and the number of days until the invoice is due (see **Figure 7-2**).

7. Click [Ctrl]+[Home] to return to cell D6 and re-orient the worksheet correctly.

8. Click on Window in the menu bar.

9. Click on Unfreeze Panes to return the worksheet to Normal View.

10. Save this worksheet as Profit2000.xls

More

When you open an existing workbook, the cell pointer is in the cell it was in when you last saved the workbook. You should get in the habit of pressing [Ctrl]+[Home] to return to cell A1 before saving your work.

Figure 7-1 Excel Worksheet with frozen window

Intersecting points mark area which will be frozen

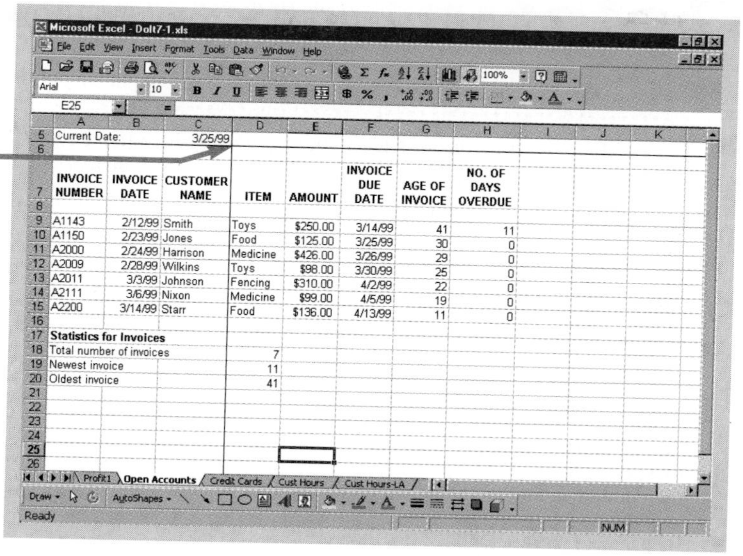

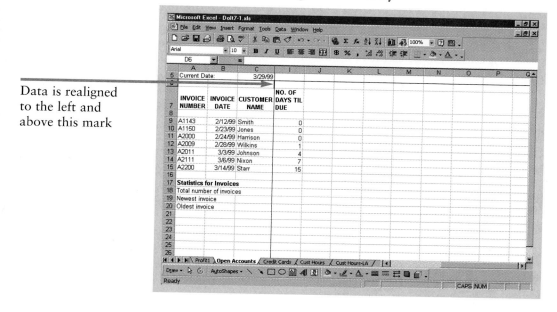

Figure 7-2 Data aligned correctly

Data is realigned to the left and above this mark

Excel 2000

Practice

Using the same worksheet, try freezing different panes to see the effect it has on scrolling to get information.

Hot Tip

You can also freeze entire rows just below their labels to scroll through a list vertically and keep the labels in place. Click on the row heading just below the labels. Use the freeze panes command. The information above the row heading is now frozen.

Inserting and Deleting Worksheets

Concept

New workbooks open with three sheets available with which to create new worksheets. Sometimes, three sheets are not enough. At other times, you may wish to delete worksheets for a variety of reasons. Excel makes it easy to do both.

Do It!

Kay is going to add a new worksheet to her workbook so that she can create a customer hours worksheet. She will also name the new worksheet.

1 Open the Student File Profit2000.xls.

2 Click on Insert on the Menu bar.

3 Scroll down to Worksheet and click on it. A new worksheet and a new tab are created in the workbook (see **Figure 7-3**).

4 Click and drag the tab of the new worksheet, labeled Sheet 4 to the right of the sheet labeled Credit Cards.

5 Right click on the new sheet label. From the pop-up menu, select Rename and click on it (see **Figure 7-4**).

6 Type Cust Hours as the new name of the worksheet.

7 Save your workbook by clicking opening the File menu and clicking Save. The Save dialog box will open.

8 Type the title, New Workbook, and click Save. In the future you can save this document, clicking File, then save, or clicking the Save icon on the Standard toolbar.

More

The Save command and Save As command perform separate functions. The first time you save a document there will be no difference between Save and Save As. Once a document exists, using the Save command will simply overwrite the existing document. The Save As command allows you to change the name of the document, and the location.

You may also move and copy worksheets from one workbook to another. To do this open the workbook which will receive the sheets. Then click on the workbook that that contains the sheets you want to copy or move, and select the sheets you want. Click Edit, then click Move or Copy Sheet. In the box which appears, the To book box, you may click on the book you are moving the sheets to or you may create a new workbook. The Before Sheet box will appear asking you to specify where you want to add the sheet. If you want to copy the sheet rather than move it, click the Create a copy check box.

Figure 7-3 New worksheet with new tab

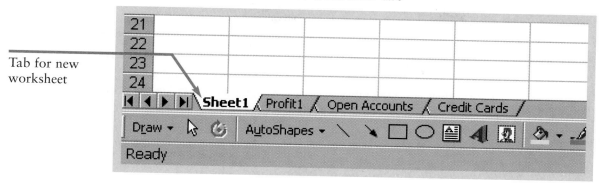

Tab for new
worksheet

Excel 2000

Figure 7-4 Selecting the Rename command

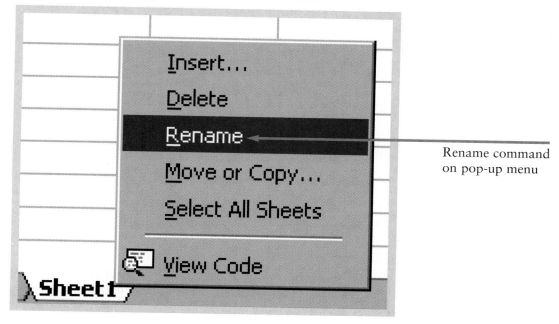

Rename command
on pop-up menu

Practice

Add two more sheets to the workbook you were just working on. Name them, as you like.

Hot Tip

You can also copy the active worksheet by clicking **Edit** on the menu bar, and clicking **Move** or **Copy Sheet**. You choose the sheet the copy will precede and then click the **Copy** check box.

Referencing Another Worksheet

Concept

At times, data you need may not be in the worksheet you are currently working on. Excel offers you the ability to reference other sheets within a workbook, and other workbooks.

Do It!

Kay has two worksheets to keep track of dog-grooming customers in her two salons. However, she has only one customer who has work done in both salons. Kay will reference one worksheet containing that customer's hours into another worksheet containing more of that customer's hours so that she has a total number of hours worked for that customer. She will also reformat the cells on a worksheet.

1 Open the File named Doit7-2.xls, and click on the Cust Hours tab to bring it forward.

2 Click on cell F16 to make it active.

3 Click on the ☰ in the toolbar.

4 Click on the Tab titled Cust Hours ñ LA to bring that worksheet forward.

5 Click on Cell F15 to add it to the formula. Notice that the formula now reads =0+'Cust Hours-LA'! F15 (see **Figure 7-5**).

6 Click ▭ OK ▭ on the Edit formula box to complete the referencing.

7 The total in Cell F16 of the Cust Hours worksheet now reads 3, and the total for the week has been updated to reflect the added hours (see **Figure 7-6**).

8 Save your work as Profit2000.xls, replacing the previous file.

More

If you know the exact cell of the worksheet you wish to reference, you can shortcut the process by using the formula bar of the worksheet where you want the information placed. Start by typing an =, then 0, then +. Following that, type the name of the worksheet you want to reference. Be sure to put the worksheet name in single quotation marks. Type an exclamation point to tell the program that this is an outside reference. Finally, type the cell number of the information and press Enter.

Figure 7-5 Referencing formula

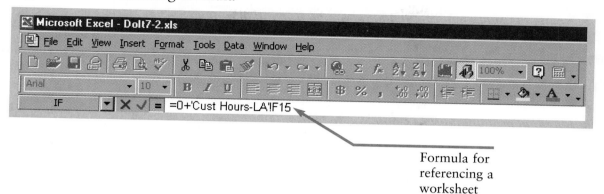

Formula for referencing a worksheet

Figure 7-6 Updated worksheet

	F16		=	=0+'Cust Hours-LA'!F15					
	A	B	C	D	E	F	G	H	I	J

Kay's Hound Accessories
Weekly Customer Summary

Weekly Customer Work Summary

	Name	Acct. Number	Monday	Tuesday	Wednesday	Thursday	Friday	Saturday	Weekly Total
7	Adams	11523	2.5	0	2.5	0	2.75	0	7.75
8	Benson	11253	0	3	0	3.5	0	3	9.5
9	Childes	12221	0	2	0	2	0	3	7
10	Dunbar	11156	3	0	3	0	2.5	0	8.5
11	Evers	13256	1.25	0	1.25	0	2	0	4.5
12	Ferris	5321	0	3	0	0	0	0	3
13	Frost	1523	2	0	2	0	2	0	6
14	Miller	25246	0	0.5	0	3.5	0	3	7
15	Stevens	18975	2	0	2	0	1.75	2.5	8.25
16	Worley	15869	2	0	2.25	3	2.25	2.5	12

Cell F16 is updated

Practice

Add a new customer with the same name and customer number to both worksheets. Create hours for that customer in both worksheets and then practice referencing the worksheets.

Hot Tip

If you need to change the data in a referenced cell, you should be aware that any changes you make would affect the cell that is relying on that data.

Saving a Worksheet as a Web Page

Concept

With the increasing influence of the World Wide Web in business, it becomes necessary know how to post data onto the Web.

Do It!

Kay will change the appearance of her worksheet, and then save it as a Web page.

1. Open Doit7-6.xls. Make sure the Profit1 worksheet is the active worksheet.

2. Click on Cell C8 then click on the Format Painter icon 🖌 on the Standard toolbar. The formatting in Cell C8 is now ready to be copied to another cell.

3. Click on Cell D8 to reformat it.

4. The information in Cell C20 should be in Cell D20. Click Cell C20, and open the Insert menu.

5. Select Cells and the Add Cells dialog box will open (see **Figure 7-7**).

6. Click on the Shift Cells Right, and then [OK]. The information is moved to the correct cell.

7. Open the File menu and select Save As.

8. Click the drop-down arrow in the Save as type: selection box and click on Web Page. The Web Page Save dialog box opens (see **Figure 7-8**)

9. Highlight the file name and change it by typing: Kay's Web Page.

10. Click Save. The worksheet is now ready to publish as a Web page.

More

If you are going to publish workbooks on the Web you may need to add hyperlinks to it. A hyperlink is a piece of text which allows people viewing the Web page to click on the hyperlink which takes them to another Web page. Click Insert, then click Hyperlink to add a hyperlink to a worksheet.

You may also send workbooks over the internet via e-mail rather than publishing it on the Web. Clicking, File, then Send to, then clicking Mail Recipient(as attachment). This function will allow you to send an e-mail to someone, and attach the workbook to that e-mail.

Before you save a worksheet as a Web page you should first preview it in Web Preview. If you click File, then Web Page Preview, your browser will open, showing you what your worksheet will look like when it is published as a web page. This will allow you to make any format changes which may be neccessary before publishing the worksheet on the Web.

Figure 7-7 Insert Cells box

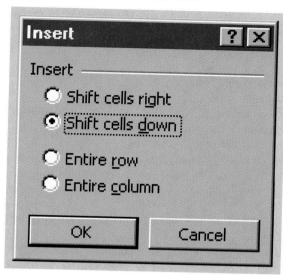

Excel 2000

Figure 7-8 Save As dialog box

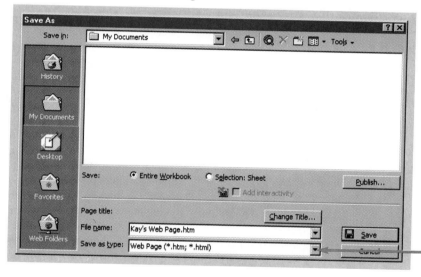

Allows you to
change the
type of file
you are saving

Practice

Using the same workbook, open the other
four tabs (**Credit Cards, Open Accounts,
Cust Hours, Cust Hours LA**) and save
them as Web pages.

Hot Tip

Using the **Change Title...** option in the Web
Page Save box allows you to pick a title for
your Web page and have it displayed in the
titlebar of the Web browser.

 # Using Headers and Footers

Concept

Headers and footers contain information at the top and bottom of pages, respectively. You can place information in headers and footers that will only appear in Print Preview, or in the printed copy.

Do It!

Kay will add a header to one of her customer hour worksheets so that she can easily differentiate between the two of them when they are printed.

1. Open your Profit2000.xls file and click on the Cust Hours tab to make it the active worksheet.

2. Click File, then click Page Setup on the menu.

3. Click on the Header/Footer tab of the Page Setup dialog box to bring it to the front (see **Figure 7-9**).

4. Click the drop down arrow in the Header text selection box.

5. Scroll down and select the title Cust Hours by clicking on it.

6. Click [OK].

7. Click on the Print Preview button 🔍 on the toolbar.

8. Notice that the worksheet in Print Preview now has the header, Cust Hours (see **Figure 7-10**).

9. Close the Print Preview window.

10. Open the Page Setup dialog box again.

11. Click the drop-down arrow in the Footer selection box.

12. Select Page 1 from the drop down box. The setup box should now look like **Figure 7-11**.

13. Click [OK].

14. Check your work in Print Preview. Save your work.

More

To change gridlines, print quality, row and column headings, or other things, access the Page Setup dialog box and click on the [Options...] button on the right side of the box.

Figure 7-9 Page Setup dialog box

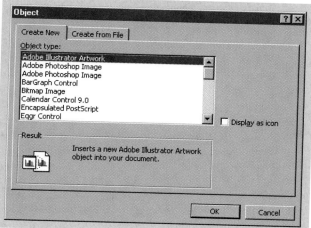

Figure 7-10 Worksheet in Print Preview

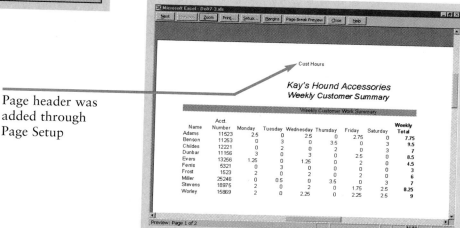

Page header was
added through
Page Setup

Figure 7-11 Header/Footer section of Setup box

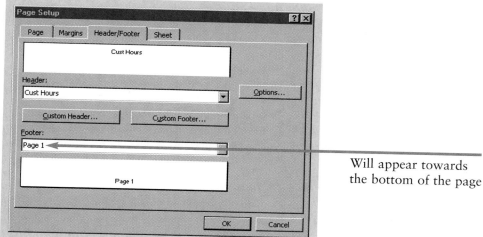

Will appear towards
the bottom of the page

Practice

Add a header and footer to the **Cust Hours-LA** worksheet. **Use Cust Hours-LA** as the title and **Page 1** as the footer. Save your work as **Profit2000.xls**.

Hot Tip

Before you print anything in Excel, you should spell check it. Simply click on the Spelling and Grammar button on the toolbar and Excel will find your mistakes and suggest corrections.

 **Creating a Custom View**

Concept

Excel allows the user to change the way a worksheet is viewed on the screen or in Print Preview. Further, you can save several views of a worksheet without having to save separate sheets under separate file names.

Do It!

Kay will name and save two separate views for her original worksheet.

1 Open your Profit2000.xls file and click on the Profit 1 tab.

2 Click View on the menu bar, and then click Custom Views. The Custom Views dialog box opens (see **Figure 7-12**).

3 Right now, there are no custom views for this worksheet. Click Add.

4 In the Add View dialog box that opens (see **Figure 7-13**), type Normal, then click OK .

5 Click once in the Zoom box on the toolbar.

6 Type 70, and then press [Enter].

7 The screen is now 70% of the original size. Click View on the menu bar, and then Custom Views.

8 Click Add.

9 In the Add View dialog box, type Layout to name the view.

10 Click OK .

11 Save your work.

More

Now that you have two views of the same worksheet, you can move between them by clicking on the Custom View option of the View menu and choosing one or the other.

Figure 7-12 Custom Views dialog box

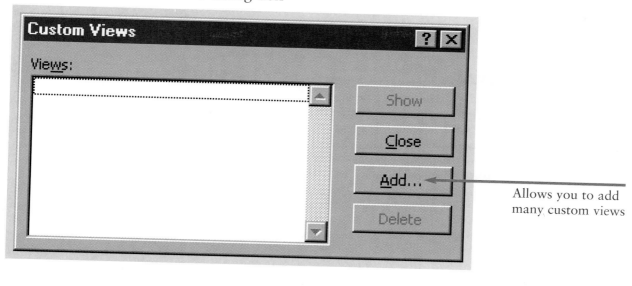

Allows you to add
many custom views

Excel 2000

Figure 7-13 Add View dialog box

Allows you to fully
customize views of the
worksheet, including
hidden rows

Practice

Using the same worksheet, create and
name a custom view of **150%**, and one of
30%.

Hot Tip

To delete views from the active worksheet,
click on **View**, then **Custom Views**. Select
the view you wish to delete, click once on
it, and press the **delete** key.

Using Page Breaks and Numbers

Concept

Excel inserts page breaks, indicated by dashed lines, whenever your worksheet has more information than can be printed on one page. You can, however, insert a manual page break wherever you wish so as to limit the amount of information printed on one page.

Do It!

Kay will insert a manual page break on her credit card worksheet so that she can print a copy of the cardholder name, and the amount they owe.

1. Open your Profit2000.xls file and click on the Credit Cards Tab.

2. Click on cell D5. This is where the page break will occur. Click on Insert on the menu bar. From the Insert menu, click on Insert Page Break.

3. Notice the dashed lines that appear on the page (see **Figure 7-14**). These indicate where the page break will be.

4. Click on the Print Preview button 🔍 on the toolbar.

5. The first page contains very little data. Scroll down until you find the page with the Name of the cardholder and the amount they owe (see **Figure 7-15**).

6. Click on Print on the Print Preview menu bar. When the Print dialog box opens (see **Figure 7-16**), click on Pages radio button in the Print range box.

7. Type the number 2 in the From: selection box. Click the To: selection box to activate it, and type 2.

8. Click [OK] to print just page 2 of the worksheet. Save your work and close the workbook. Close the Print View.

9. Click on Insert in the menu bar. Click on Remove Page Break.

10. Save your work.

More

If you don't see the page breaks inserted by Excel, click Tools on the menu bar, then Options, then the View tab. Check to make sure the page breaks check box is selected.

You may also want to rotate the text or apply styles to your worksheet if you want to format it before you print. To rotate text, you must click Format, then Cells. On the Alignment tab you can adjust the angle of the text by changing the number of degrees on the right side of the box.

You may create your own styles and apply them, by clicking Format, then Style. In the Style diaolg box click the Modify button. The Format Cells dialog box appears, allowing you to create your own styles. Then you may apply these styles using the Formatting toolbar in Excel.

Figure 7-14 Dashed lines indicate page break

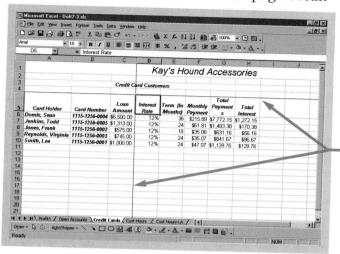

Dashed lines mark
the page breaks

Figure 7-15 First page with little data

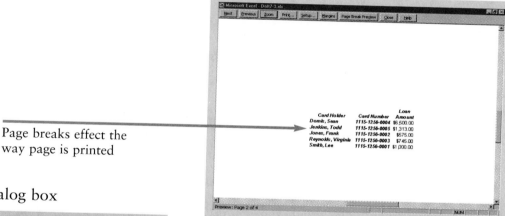

Page breaks effect the
way page is printed

Figure 7-16 Print dialog box

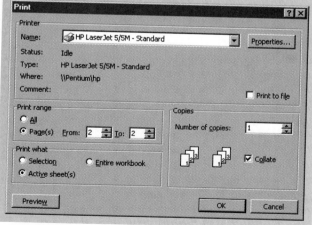

Practice

Using the same worksheet, insert page breaks at three different spots on the worksheet, and then move to Print Preview to see the effect.

Hot Tip

If you want to manually adjust the page breaks, you can click on **Page Break Preview** in the Print Preview window. This allows you to customize the page breaks by clicking and dragging them.

Adjusting Page Setup

Concept

The Page setup feature of Excel allows the user to alter the appearance of a printed document by centering the document on the page, changing the left and right margins, and changing the sizes of the header and footer.

Do It!

Kay will alter the second page of the document listing just customer name and credit card amount due.

1. Open your Profit2000.xls file and click on the Credit Cards tab to bring it forward.

2. Click on cell D4 and insert a page break.

3. Click on the Print Preview button 🔍 on the Standard toolbar.

4. Once in Print Preview, scroll down until page 2 is on the screen.

5. Click on Margins. Now, you can see the margins on the screen and the location of the header and footer (see **Figure 7-17**). Click on Setup.

6. Click to bring the Margins tab to the front.

7. For this small amount of information, the margins are acceptable. However, click on the Center on Page, Vertically and Horizontally check boxes to select them.

8. Click the Header/Footer tab to bring it to the front.

9. Click on the drop-down arrow in the Header selection box. Scroll down and select the title Credit Cards.

10. Click [OK] to view the changes. Your page should now look like **Figure 7-18**.

11. Click Print.

12. In the Print dialog box click the Page(s) option selection box.

13. Type 2 in both boxes so that only page 2 is printed.

14. Click [OK] to print page 2.

15. Close the Print Preview and save the changes.

More

You can preview your worksheet and see what it would look like as a Web page. By opening the file menu and clicking on the Preview as Webpage option, Excel will open your Web browser and show you the worksheet as it would appear on the World Wide Web.

Figure 7-17 Margins visible in Print Preview

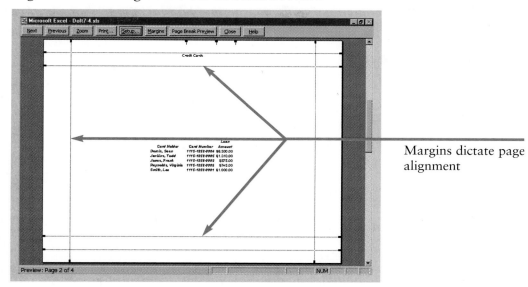

Margins dictate page
alignment

Excel 2000

Figure 7-18 Page realigned in Print Preview

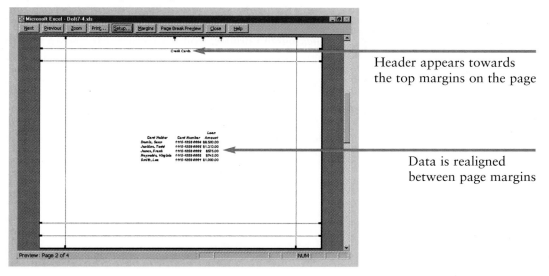

Header appears towards
the top margins on the page

Data is realigned
between page margins

Practice

Change the page break on this worksheet, and then in Print Preview mode, click and drag the margins and headers and footers to see the effect such actions have.

Hot Tip

Clicking the **Options** button in the Print dialog box will give you four more options concerning printing. They are: **Paper size**, **print quality**, **font type**, and **device** options.

 # Inserting an Object into a Worksheet

Concept

Excel gives you the power to insert objects into worksheets, and move those objects.

Do It!

Kay will insert a picture into one of her worksheets.

1 Open Doit7-5.xls and click on the Cust Hours tab to bring that worksheet forward.

2 Open the Insert menu and click on Object. The Insert Object dialog box opens (see **Figure 7-19**).

3 Scroll through the Create New selection box until you find Microsoft Clip Gallery. Double-click on it to open the clip gallery.

4 Type dog in the Search for Clips box (see **Figure 7-20**).

5 When the picture appears, click on it. A small gray box with four icons appears.

6 Click on the top icon to insert the picture into the worksheet.

7 By clicking and dragging on the picture, Move it so that the top lines up with the bottom of row 17 and the left side is flush against the margin.

8 Click on any cell to set the picture in place.

More

To delete a picture from a worksheet, click once on it to select it, and then press the delete key.

Figure 7-19 Insert Object dialog box

Different galleries
of images

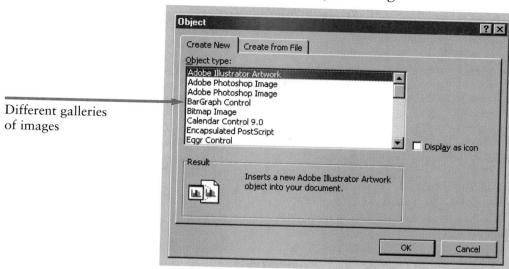

Figure 7-20 Microsoft Clip Gallery

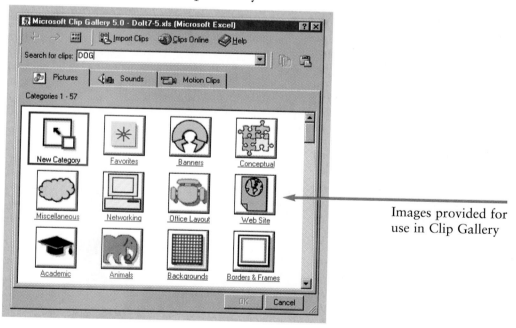

Images provided for
use in Clip Gallery

Practice

Remove the picture of the dog from the
worksheet, and select another from the
Microsoft Clip Gallery. Insert it, move it, set
it, and delete it.

Hot Tip

Using the Clips Online option in the
Microsoft Clip Gallery allows you to
connect to the World Wide Web to find
more pictures to insert.

Shortcuts

Function	Button/Mouse	Menu	Keyboard
Print		Click File, then click Print	[Ctrl]+[P]
Print Preview		Click File, then click Print Preview	
Page Break Preview		Click View, then Page Break Preview	
Normal View		Click View, then click Normal	
Save as Web Page		Click File, then Save as Web Page	
Set Print Area		Click File, then click Set Print Area	

Quiz

Identify Key Features

Name the items indicated by callouts in **Figure 7-21**.

Figure 7-21 Elements of the Excel worksheet

Excel 2000

Select The Best Answer

9. Indicates a page break.

10. This command will cause a section of the screen to remain immobile.

11. Click on this command first to add a worksheet to a workbook.

12. Using data from one worksheet in another worksheet is called this.

13. When you secure an entire workbook, you will need this to open it.

14. A header is located on this part of the page.

15. This part of the Standard toolbar gives you the size of the active window expressed as a percentage.

16. In Print Preview, the margins of each page become visible when you click on this button.

a. Margins

b. Zoom

c. Top

d. Bottom

e. Insert

f. Referencing

g. Password

h. Dashed Line

i. Freeze Command

Quiz (continued)

Complete the Statement

17. The frozen areas of a worksheet are called:

    a. Columns

    b. Rows

    c. Panes

    d. Cells

18. The number of worksheets a new workbook opens with is:

    a. 4

    b. 3

    c. 2

    d. 1

19. Using data from one worksheet in another worksheet is called:

    a. Freezing

    b. Printing

    c. Saving

    d. Referencing

20. You can hide all the formulas in a worksheet by selecting a group of cells, and using the option:

    a. Format Cells

    b. Freeze Windows

    c. Print Preview

    d. Page Break

21. A special place for holding information at the bottom of a page is called a:

    a. Tab

    b. Scroll bar

    c. Header

    d. Footer

22. If you change the way a worksheet is viewed on the screen, or in print preview, you can save the view using the:

    a. Format cells dialog box

    b. Format worksheet dialog box

    c. Add a View dialog box

    d. Print Preview dialog box

23. Whenever your worksheet has more information than can be printed on one page, Excel inserts:

    a. Column Indicators

    b. Row Breaks

    c. Page Breaks

    d. None of the above

24. To alter the appearance of a printed document, use the:

    a. Save As

    b. Page Setup

    c. Close button

    d. View Toolbars

Interactivity

Test Your Skills

1. Freeze columns and rows:

a. Open the Student file Doit7-1.xls. Save it as Practice 7.

b. Make the Cust Hours worksheet active.

c. Freeze columns A and B, and rows 6-15. (Hint: click on cell C6 first.)

d. Scroll to the right until the Account Number and Weekly Totals columns are next to one another. Unfreeze the panes.

2. Copy a worksheet:

a. Make the Cust Hours-LA worksheet active. Right click active worksheet tab.

b. Select Move or Copy. Create a copy and move it to the end.

c. Delete the new worksheet.

3. Insert a page break:

a. Make the Profit 1 worksheet the active worksheet. Click cell I21.

b. Insert a page break. Change to Print Preview.

c. Print your worksheet. Undo the page break.

4. Reference worksheet data:

a. Click on the Cust Hours-LA tab and click on cell D10. Click the equal sign ▣ in the formula bar.

b. Click the Cust hours tab.

c. Click on Cell D12 (click and drag the Edit Formula box if it's in the way). Press [Enter].

5. Adjusting Page Setup:

a. Make the Credit Card worksheet active.

b. Go to Print Preview. Go to Set Up.

c. Click the Margins tab.

d. Make the left and right margins both 1, and center the document both vertically and horizontally.

e. Print the document.

Interactivity (continued)

Problem Solving

Kay Samoy is your customer. You have created the worksheets for her and have kept track of all the data contained therein. Kay would like several reports from you containing specific data. Make a copy of only the Pie Chart from the Profit 1 worksheet, centered in the middle of the page. To do this you will have to manipulate margins in the Page Setup and Print Preview modes of Excel.

You must also make a copy of the Open Accounts worksheet with only the Invoice number, Invoice date, Customer name, and Amount. Use the Hide and Unhide commands to perform this task.

Kay has also asked for a copy of all the credit card information, including appropriate labels for Sean Domis. You should use the freeze window command to isolate and move the data you are looking for. Make sure you print only the information you have been asked to.

Finally, Kay would like a copy of the weekly customer hours for the LA salon with the header **Customer Hours ñ LA**. Add a Header in the Page Setup dialog box to add a header to this page.

Make these copies and print them with the appropriate footer indicating page numbers. For every page you create add a footer, and number the pages in the footer in the order which they were asked for, and printed.

L E S S O N

WORKING WITH LISTS

A s we have seen in previous lessons, the main function of the Excel program is to create spreadsheets. Spreadsheets are a highly organized and efficient means to track business expenses, and chart the future course of businesses.

At some point, a business will probably need to create a file or a group of files with information about customers or their buying habits. These files are called databases. See **Figure 8-1** which is a database created with **Microsoft Access**. A database is a collection of information about any particular subject. For example, a phone-book is a database; so is a catalog.

Even though Excel is a spreadsheet program, you can use it to create simple databases. In Excel, a database is called a list. Using an Excel list, you can organize and manage worksheet information so that you can quickly find needed data for projects, charts, and reports.

Case Study:
Kay will make a list of her best customers, so she can remember who to send thank you notes too. She will include their names, addresses and how much they spend.

Introduction to Lists

Concept

Planning a list is a lot like planning anything else in Excel: the "Five P" method applies. In other words, "Proper Planning Prevents Poor Performance." When planning a list, you must consider the kind of information the list will contain, and how you will work with that information now, and in the future.

Kay's business is doing quite well, due mainly to the repeat business of her customers. She decides to thank her customers using a mass mailing. To do this mass mailing, she will create a list of her most valued customers.

Kay must first identify the purpose of the list. She takes out a piece of paper and at the top, writes "List of Valued Customers to send thank you card." Now, she knows that the purpose of the list is to create a database of names and addresses of repeat customers.

Next, she must determine the structure of her list. In this case, and in many cases, the purpose of the list will determine its structure. Since this is a list for mailing, Kay can easily identify the fields that she needs. Under the top line on the piece of paper, she writes, "Name," "Street," "City," "State," and "Zip," and "Amount spent." With this last column, she will determine to whom to send cards.

A final consideration for Kay would be to determine if any special formatting is required in the list. Kay realizes that some of the zip codes in her area have zeros in them. She knows that Excel eliminates zeros at the beginning of numbers. However, she also knows that adding an apostrophe to the beginning of numbers will tell Excel not to do this. She makes a note to add apostrophes to zip codes beginning with zero. See **Figure 8-2** for Kay's completed list.

Another determination you should make concerning your list is the actual amount of data that it will contain. If your list will contain more than 65,536 records, you would be better off using database software like Access 2000 rather than spread-sheet software.

When you create a new workbook, Excel also provides you with templates which may be used to fill out the structure of the type of workbook you want to create. Some of these templates may have to be loaded from the Office 2000 installation CD. Templates provide you with an outline; it is up to you to fill in the information which makes up the workbook.

Figure 8-1 A database

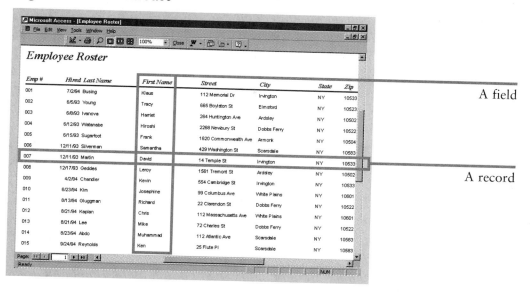

Microsoft Access - [Employee Roster]
Employee Roster
A field
A record

Emp #	Hired	Last Name	First Name	Street	City	State	Zip
001	7/2/94	Busing	Klaus	112 Memorial Dr	Irvington	NY	10533
002	6/5/93	Young	Tracy	665 Boylston St	Elmsford	NY	10523
003	6/8/93	Ivanova	Harriet	264 Huntington Ave	Ardsley	NY	10502
004	6/12/93	Watanabe	Hiroshi	2268 Newbury St	Dobbs Ferry	NY	10522
005	6/15/93	Sugarfoot	Frank	1620 Commonwealth Ave	Armonk	NY	10504
006	12/11/93	Silverman	Samantha	429 Washington St	Scarsdale	NY	10583
007	12/11/93	Martin	David	14 Temple St	Irvington	NY	10533
008	12/17/93	Geddes	Leroy	1561 Tremont St	Ardsley	NY	10502
009	4/2/94	Chandler	Kevin	554 Cambridge St	Irvington	NY	10533
010	6/23/94	Kim	Josephine	99 Columbus Ave	White Plains	NY	10601
011	8/13/94	Gluggman	Richard	22 Clarendon St	Dobbs Ferry	NY	10522
012	8/21/94	Kaplan	Chris	112 Massachusetts Ave	White Plains	NY	10601
013	8/21/94	Lee	Mike	72 Charles St	Dobbs Ferry	NY	10522
014	8/23/94	Abdo	Muhammad	112 Atlantic Ave	Scarsdale	NY	10583
015	9/24/94	Reynolds	Ken	25 Flute Pl	Scarsdale	NY	10583

Figure 8-2 Planning a list

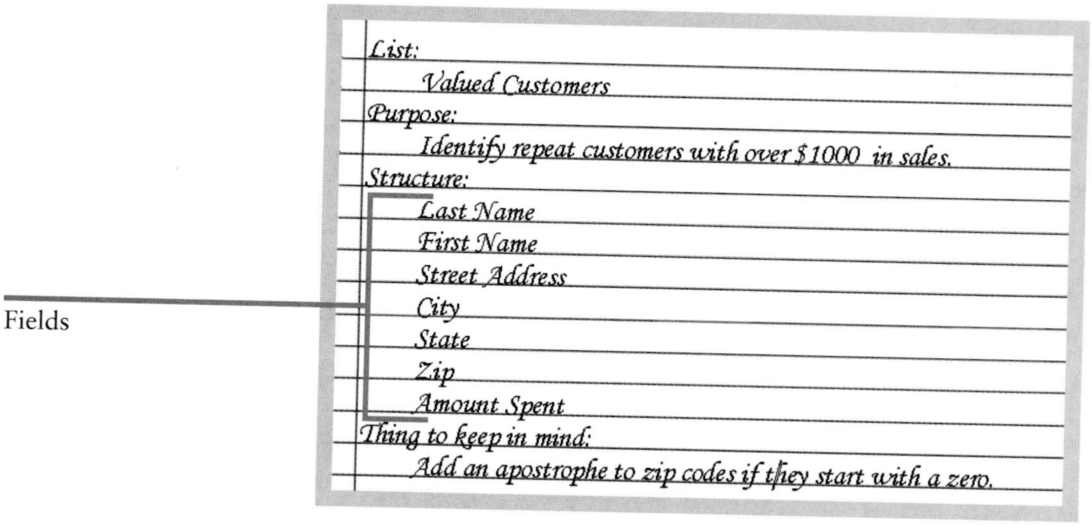

List:
Valued Customers
Purpose:
Identify repeat customers with over $1000 in sales.
Structure:
Last Name
First Name
Street Address
City
State
Zip
Amount Spent
Thing to keep in mind:
Add an apostrophe to zip codes if they start with a zero.
Fields

Practice

Using a sheet of paper, construct your own list of people to solicit money from for a new business venture. Determine the purpose of the list and the fields to include.

Hot Tip

Two important parts of a list to remember are **Records** and **Fields**. Records contain data about an object or person. Fields describe the characteristics about the records, such as name or address. Fields occurs in Columns. Records occur in rows.

Constructing a List

Concept

Field names allow you to organize the information in your list. Field names may be up to 255 characters in length.

Do It!

Kay will begin creating her list by entering the names of the fields on her worksheet.

1   Open Student File Doit8-1.xls.

2   Click cell A1 to activate it, and type the name of the first field, Last Name.

3   Click Cell B1 to activate it. Type First Name in this cell.

4   In cell C1, type Street Address.

5   In cell D1, type City.

6   In cell E1, type State.

7   In cell F1, type Zip Code.

8   In cell G1, type Amount Spent. Your list should match the one in **Figure 8-3**.

9   Notice that parts of some field names are hidden because they are too long for the column (see **Figure 8-4**). To correct this, click on cell A1 first.

10 While holding down the [Ctrl] key, click on the other labels that are too long (cells B1, C1, and G1). Your list should now resemble **Figure 8-5**.

Figure 8-3 Worksheet with database fields

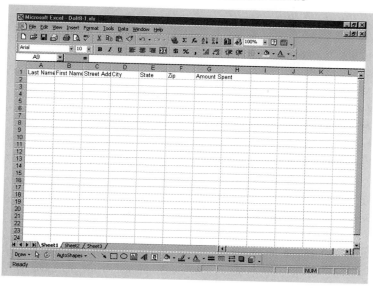

Figure 8-4 Not all field names fit

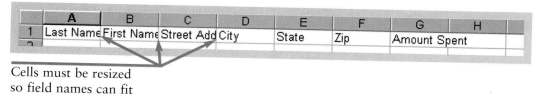

Cells must be resized
so field names can fit

Figure 8-5 Cells are selected

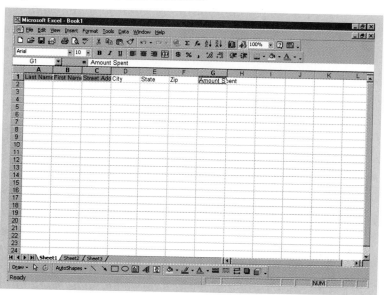

Constructing a list (continued)

Do It

11 Now, click on Format in the menu bar.

12 Rest the mouse pointer over the word column in the menu, and when the submenu opens, click on Autofit Selection (see **Figure 8-6**). The columns expand to reveal the labels (see **Figure 8-7**).

13 Select cells A1-G1 using the click and drag method.

14 Click on the Bold option in the Formatting toolbar.

15 Click on the down arrow of the Borders button on the Formatting toolbar.

16 Click on the Bottom Double Borders option. This is the first selection in the second row. Your list should now look like **Figure 8-8**.

17 Save your work as Valued Customer List.xls.

More

To protect the integrity of your list, make sure the data is entered in the correct field. You should stress consistency and care to anyone who is entering information into a list. If you enter data incorrectly, it will adversely affect the result of any manipulations of the list.

Figure 8-6 Column submenu

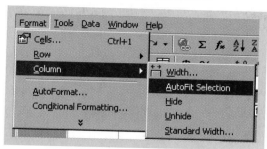

Figure 8-7 Cells are resized so field names fit

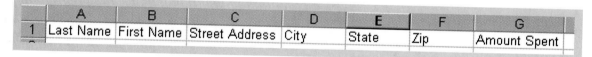

Figure 8-8 Field names are now formatted

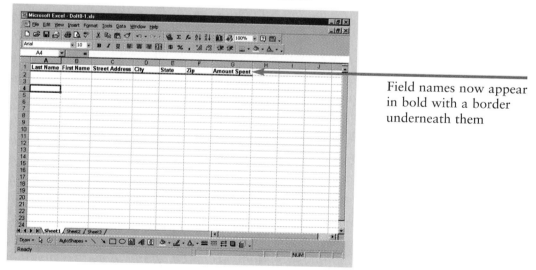

Field names now appear
in bold with a border
underneath them

Practice

Open student practice file **Prac8-2.xls** and
follow the instructions.

Hot Tip

If the field name you plan to use is wider
than the data in the column, you can use
the **Wrap Text** option in the **Format Cells**
dialog box.

Excel 2000

Entering Records with the Data Form

Concept

While it is possible to enter all the information in a list directly on the list itself, there is an easier way. By using the Form function you can create a data form that allows you to enter data faster and more efficiently.

Do It!

Kay will access and use the data form to begin entering information in her list.

1 Open your file named Valued Customer List.xls and make sure cell A1 is active.

2 Click on Data in the menu bar, and then click on Form. The message you see on the screen asks you if you'd like to select the first row as the labels for your form (see **Figure 8-9**). Click [OK].

3 The form is now on the screen with the last name field active (see **Figure 8-10**). Type Smith in the last name field and press the [Tab] key once.

4 Type Michael in the first name field. Enter the rest of the information, 123 Adams Street, Boston, MA, 12231, $1500 in each succeeding text box by using the [Tab] key.

5 When you finish entering the information, press [Enter].

6 Enter each of the following customers using the Data Form:

Jones, Kim, 105 South Street, Baytown, MA, 12322, $700.
Donne, John, 23 Main Street, Cambridge, MA, 12222, $1250.
Harris, Phil, 1200 Avenue C, Malden, MA, 13444, $450.
Magritte, Rene, 234 Rouge Ave, Boston, MA, 12231, $2000.

7 Save your work as Valued Customer List.xls.

More

The scroll bar on the data form allows you to scroll through the records in the list. Clicking on the down arrow will take you to the next record in the list, and clicking on the up arrow will take you to the previous record.

Figure 8-9 Excel warning box

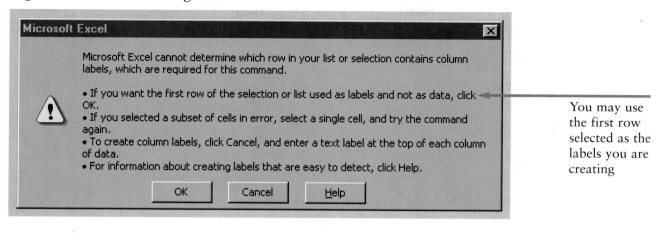

Microsoft Excel cannot determine which row in your list or selection contains column labels, which are required for this command.

• If you want the first row of the selection or list used as labels and not as data, click OK.
• If you selected a subset of cells in error, select a single cell, and try the command again.
• To create column labels, click Cancel, and enter a text label at the top of each column of data.
• For information about creating labels that are easy to detect, click Help.

OK   Cancel   Help

You may use the first row selected as the labels you are creating

Excel 2000

Figure 8-10 Data form

Sheet1

Last Name:
First Name:
Street Address:
City:
State:
Zip Code:
Amount Spent:

New Record
New
Delete
Restore
Find Prev
Find Next
Criteria
Close

Adds records to database

Practice

Enter the following customers on the Valued Customer list: **Sam Watson, Framingham, MA, 222 Black Street, $500. 13345. June Cleaver, $300, Cambridge, MA. 34 Long Street**. Save your work as **Valued Customer List.xls**.

Hot Tip

Instead of using the scroll bars on the data form, you can use the arrow keys on the keyboard to move between records.

Searching for a Record

Concept

An easy way to search for records in a list is to use the **data form**. The criteria option of this form allows you to select specific items to search for.

Do It!

Kay would like to find out how many customers so far have spent over $500. She will use the data form to do this.

1. Open the file Valued Customer List.xls. Click on cell A10 and then click on Data in the menu bar.

2. Click on Form to open the data form.

3. Click on Criteria in the data form.

4. On the blank form that appears, place the insertion point in the Amount Spent text box.

5. Type >500 (see **Figure 8-11**).

6. Click Find Next to find the first record. The data form should look like **Figure 8-12**.

7. Click Find Next until you find all the records.

8. Return the form to normal by clicking Criteria and deleting the text in the Amount Spent text box.

More

You may also use the Find command to search for records which contain specific information. Click Edit, then click Find and you will be able to use the Find and Replace dialog box to search for the information you are looking for. There is also a replace tab on the dialog box which alows you to find a specific piece of data and then replace it with another piece of data you specify.

Figure 8-11 Data form with search criteria

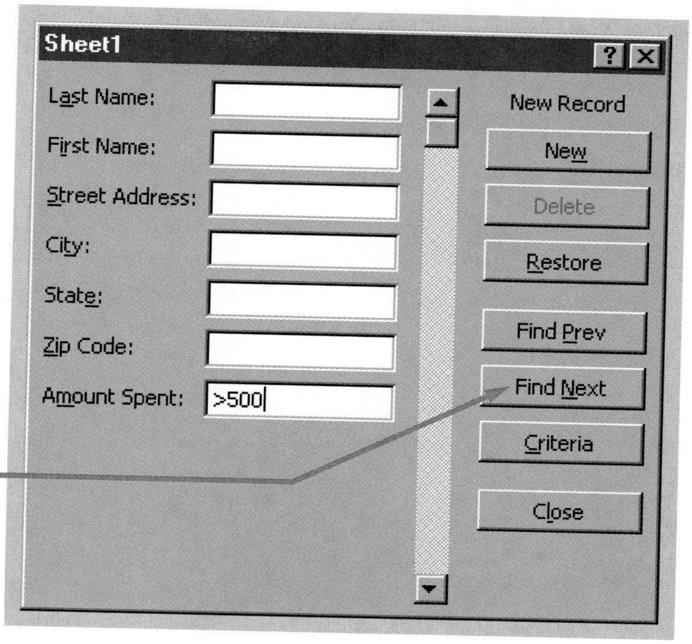

Sheet1

Last Name:	
First Name:	
Street Address:	
City:	
State:	
Zip Code:	
Amount Spent:	>500

New Record

New
Delete
Restore

Find Prev
Find Next
Criteria
Close

Allows you to search for existing records, rather than creating new ones

Excel 2000

Figure 8-12 Record which met criteria

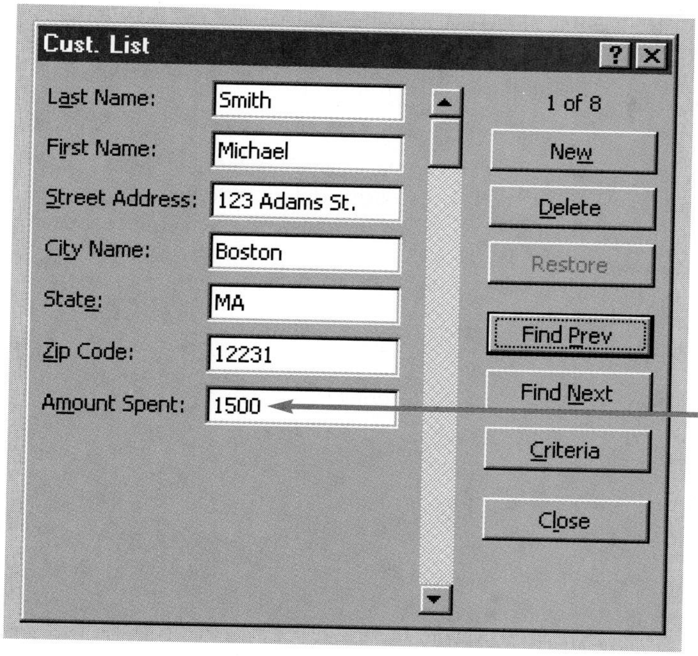

Cust. List

Last Name:	Smith
First Name:	Michael
Street Address:	123 Adams St.
City Name:	Boston
State:	MA
Zip Code:	12231
Amount Spent:	1500

1 of 8

New
Delete
Restore
Find Prev
Find Next
Criteria
Close

Any record which meets specified criteria will be found

Practice

Use the **Criteria** button on the data form to find the people living in **Cambridge**. Separately, find the people who spent less than **$500**.

Hot Tip

You can use special symbols called **Wildcards** when searching. The wildcard **?** will replace any letter or number in a series. Excel will match the numbers or letters which appear around the wildcard.

Deleting A Record

Concept

Occasionally, mistakes are going to be made entering data and data will become outdated. In these cases, you must delete records from your list.

Do It!

Kay notices that she has a duplicate record in her list. She will delete the record using the data form.

1. Open your Valued Customer List.xls file.

2. Click Data on the menu bar and then click Form.

3. Scroll through the records using the arrow keys.

4. Scroll back until you find the first entry for Kim Jones (see **Figure 8-13**).

5. Click the Delete button on the form.

6. A warning appears on the screen telling you the displayed record will be permanently deleted (see **Figure 8-14**).

7. Click OK.

8. Save your work.

More

Besides using the data form to add, delete, and search for records, you can also use it to edit records. Find the record that needs to be edited, and select the text box you wish to edit.

Figure 8-13 Record selected

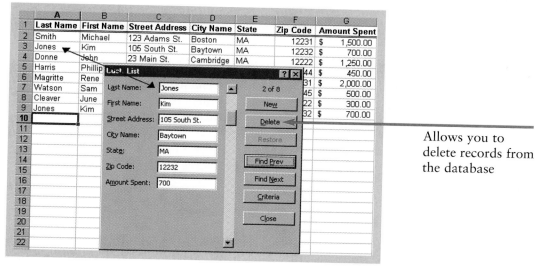

Allows you to
delete records from
the database

Figure 8-14 Excel warning box

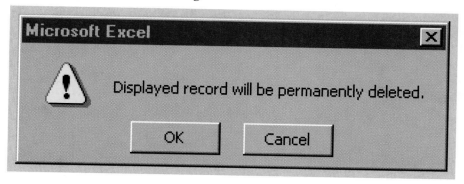

Practice

Use the form box to practice adding and deleting records. Add at least two records to the list and then delete them.

Hot Tip

Remember once you delete a record, you cannot retrieve it. Clicking **Restore** on the data form will not restore deleted records.

Sorting a List

Concept

Normally, records are entered in the order they are received rather than in alphabetical or numerical order. Therefore, Excel offers you the option of sorting your entire list based on criteria that you select.

Do It!

Kay will sort her list by the amount each customer spent first, and then alphabetically.

1 Open your Valued Customer List.xls file.

2 Click on Data in the menu bar, and then click Sort. The Sort dialog box opens (see **Figure 8-15**).

3 Click on the drop-down arrow in the Sort by selection box, scroll down, and click on Amount Spent to select it.

4 Click the Descending radio button next to the Sort by selection box.

5 Click the drop-down arrow in the Then by selection box, and click on Last Name.

6 Click the Ascending radio button next to the Then by selection box.

7 Check to make sure your Sort dialog box is the same as **Figure 8-16**. Click [OK] to run the sort.

8 Save your work.

More

Sorting a list will not insure that new records entered into it will be placed according to the sort criteria. That being the case, it is advisable to sort your list whenever you add a certain number of records, or whenever a certain time period goes by. In other words, you can sort after every fifty records, or sort once a month.

Figure 8-15 Sort dialog box

Changes the order by
which fields are sorted

Once the first criteria
has been met, secondary
criteria are sorted

Excel 2000

Figure 8-16 Sort dialog box filled out

Practice

Using the same list, practice sorting by the
following fields only: **First Name, Zip Code,
City**. Do not save after any sort.

Hot Tip

If, for some reason, your sort does not turn
out the way you intended it to, press
[Ctrl]+[Z] to undo the sort and try it again.

Printing a List

Concept

While printing a list in Excel is much like printing anything else in Excel, you can add titles and formats to your list to make it look more professional.

Do It!

Kay will print her list with a print title and a new format.

1. Open the file Valued Customer List.xls.

2. Click on the Print Preview button 🔍 on the Standard toolbar.

3. Click on Setup on the menu bar in Print Preview.

4. Click on the Header/Footer tab to bring it forward and then click on Custom Header (see **Figure 8-17**).

5. Place the insertion bar in the center window of the Header dialog box that appears and click once.

6. Click on the Font button 🅰.

7. Select font style Bold Italic by clicking on its name in the font selection box. Select size 14 font by clicking on 14 in its box. Click [OK].

8. Type Valued Customer List, and click [OK].

9. Click [OK] in the Page Setup dialog box. Your list should now look like **Figure 8-18**.

Figure 8-17 Header dialog box

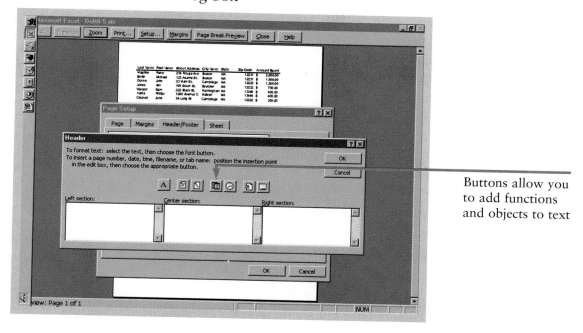

Buttons allow you
to add functions
and objects to text

Figure 8-18 Valued Customer List

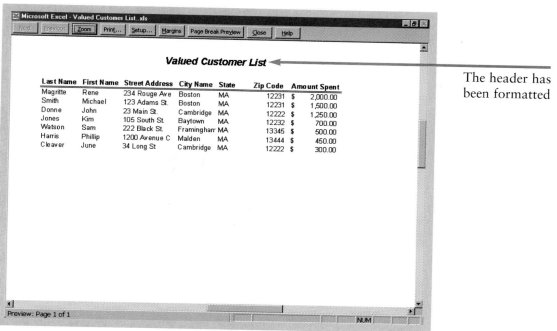

The header has
been formatted

Printing a List
(continued)

Do It!

10 Click Close to return to Normal View.

11 Click Format from the menu bar, and click on AutoFormat.

12 With the Autoformat window open (see **Figure 8-19**), scroll down the list of available formats until you see List 3. Double-click on it to select it.

13 Click on the Print Preview button 🔍 to see the change (see **Figure 8-20**).

14 Click on the Print button 🖨 to print the list.

15 Click and Drag the pointer so that the first two records in the list are selected.

16 Click File, then click Print Area. Then click Set Print Area. A dotted line will mark the first two records.

17 Print the page again, and only the records you selected will be printed.

18 Save your work.

More

If you only want to print one or several records in a list you may use the Selection command on the Print dialog box. It is a radio button, which, when clicked, will print only the cells and objects which have been selected in a worksheet.

There are several printing options which may be changed before printing begins. For example, the cell gridlines may be erased by clicking Tools, then Options. Then under Window Options on the View tab, clear the Gridlines check box, and the cell gridlines will disappear.

Figure 8-19 AutoFormat window in Excel

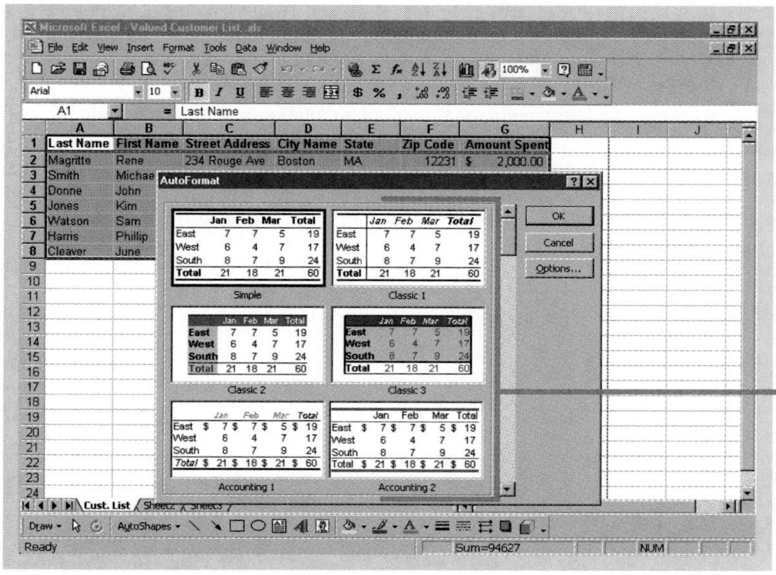

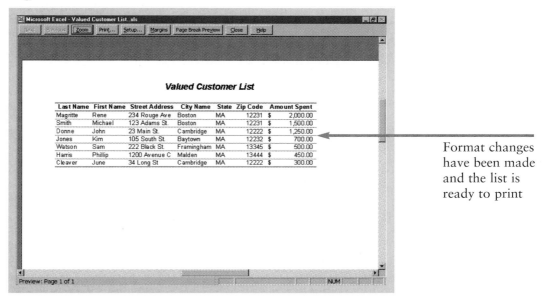

Allows you to select format changes to the list you created

Figure 8-20 List in Print Preview

Format changes have been made and the list is ready to print

Excel 2000

Practice

Using the same worksheet, practice changing the **AutoFormat** and switching between Normal and Print Preview to see the effect it has on both screens.

Hot Tip

Remember to check your list for dashed lines that indicate the margins of the page. If your table is too wide for the default Portrait view, try changing the view to Landscape in the Page tab of the Page Setup dialog box.

Shortcuts

Function	Button/Mouse	Menu	Keyboard
Sort Data		Click Data, then click Sort	
Find		Click Edit, then click Find	[Ctrl]+[F]
Print		Click File, then click Print	[Ctrl]+[P]
Print Preview		Click File, then click Print Preview	
Delete Rows		Click Edit, then click Delete, then Entire Row	
Delete Columns		Click Edit, then click Delete, then Entire Column	

Identify Key Features

Name the items indicated by callouts in **Figure 8-21**.

Figure 8-21 Excel list

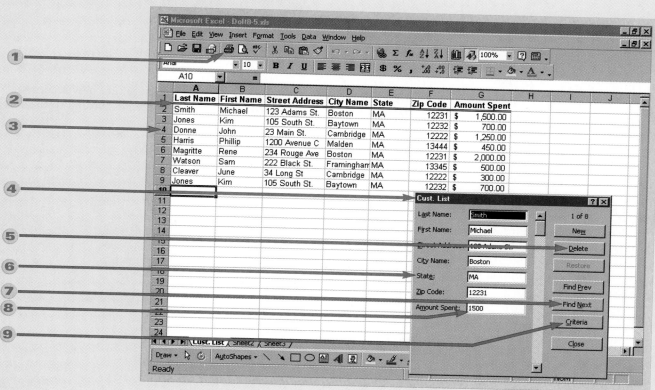

Select The Best Answer

10. Arrange records in a particular sequence.

11. Type of software used for lists too large for Excel.

12. The label at the top of a column identifying the data in that column.

13. These contain data about an object or person.

14. This is one way to enter data into a list.

15. This option allows you to select specific items to search for in a list.

a. Sort

b. Database

c. Field name

d. Records

e. Data form

f. Criteria

g. Ascending

Quiz (continued)

Complete the Statement

16. Before constructing a list, you must first identify these:

    a. Form, Content.

    b. Purpose, Structure.

    c. Parameters, Margins.

    d. Name, Number of Pages.

17. The things that allow you to sort data in your list are called:

    a. Databases

    b. Rows

    c. Fields

    d. Cells

18. To create a data form, you must first open this menu:

    a. Cell

    b. Row

    c. Kitchen

    d. Data

19. To move through the records in a list using the data form, click on the:

    a. Scroll bar

    b. Arrow Keys

    c. Print Preview

    d. Field Names

20. In order to use the data form to select specific items to search for, you must select this option:

    a. Close

    b. Criteria

    c. Delete

    d. New

21. Sorting a list _____ insure that new records entered into it will be placed according to the sort criteria.

    a. might

    b. might not

    c. will not

    d. will

22. A title for your list should be placed in the:

    a. Footer

    b. Header

    c. Margin

    d. Bottom

23. To change the entire look of your list, use this option:

    a. Theme

    b. Borders and Shading

    c. AutoFormat

    d. Bulleting

Interactivity

Test Your Skills

1. Enter new data into your list:

    a. Open the Doit8-2.xls file.

    b. Click on Data in the menu bar.

    c. Click on Form.

    d. Add this record: Steven Smith, 122 Boyle Way, Boston, MA 12234, $1500.

    e. Save your work.

2. Deleting a record:

    a. Open Student file Doit8-2.xls.

    b. Open the data form.

    c. Find the record for Steven Smith and delete it.

3. Searching for records:

    a. Open Student file Doit8-2.xls.

    b. Open the data form.

    c. Click criteria.

    d. Find all the records with under $1000 spent.

4. Sorting a list:

    a. Open Student file Doit8-2.xls.

    b. Click Data, then click Sort.

    c. Sort by Zip Code in Descending order.

    d. Do not save your work.

Problem Solving

Your company has given you the task of creating a list of employees who are close to retirement. They want the names, hire dates, birth dates, employee numbers, and months until retirement. Create a list with these criteria.

Select three separate fields to use to sort the list you create. Also alternate between sorting in descending and ascending order.

Delete several records record from your list. First use the Find Next feature to find the records whose last names begin with S. Once you have found these records delete all of the records of people whose last names begin with the letter S.

Finally view your document in Print Preview. Change the formats, and add a header to the list called, Personal List. Bold, and Italicize the header. Finally print the list.

Glossary

A

Absolute cell reference
A cell reference that will remain fixed, even if the formula containing the reference is moved. To make a cell reference absolute, place a dollar sign ($), before both the column letter and row number.

Active cell
The currently selected cell on a worksheet, indicated by the cell pointer.

Alignment
The horizontal position of values or labels within a cell (for example, left, right, or center).

Anchor cells
The first and last cells in a cell range; the cells used to express a range address (for example, B9:E9).

Animated border
Indicates that a cell's contents have been sent to the Clipboard.

Answer Wizard tab
A Help tab that allows you to ask questions about Excel topics, much like the Office Assistant.

Argument
Information such as a cell address, range, or value, enclosed in parentheses, used by a function or macro to produce a result.

Arithmetic operators
Symbols used by Excel to perform formula calculations such as +,-,*, and /.

Assumption
A variable factor that is useful for conducting What-If analysis in a worksheet.

AutoCalculate box
Automatically displays the total of the values in a selected group of cells in the status bar.

AutoComplete
Automatically finishes entering a label when its first letter(s) match that of a label used previously in the column.

AutoFill
Automatically fills a range with series information such as the days of the week when the range after the first value is selected using the fill handle.

AutoFormat
Adds a predesigned set of formatting to selected ranges. AutoFormats can modify numbers, borders, fonts, patterns, alignment, and the height and width of rows and columns.

AutoSum
A function that automatically adds the values in the cells directly above or to the left of the active cell.

C

Cancel button
Removes the contents of a cell and restores the cell's previous contents if there were any; marked by an **X** on the formula bar.

Cell
The space formed by the intersection of a row and a column; the basic unit of a worksheet.

Cell address
A cell's identification code, composed of the letter and number of the column and row that intersect to form the cell (for example, B22).

Cell pointer
The black rectangle that outlines the active cell.

Cell reference
A cell address used to refer to a cell in a formula. Cell references can be relative or absolute.

Chart
A graphic representation of values and their relationships, used to identify trends and contrasts in data.

Chart Wizard
A series of specialized dialog boxes that guide you through the creation or modification of a chart.

Check box
A small square box that allows you to turn a dialog box option on or off by clicking it.

Clipboard
A temporary storage area for cut or copied text or graphics. You can paste the contents of the Clipboard into any cell, worksheet, or even another application file. The Windows Clipboard holds a piece of information until it is replaced by another piece of data, or until the computer is shut down. The Office Clipboard holds up to twelve pieces of data at once and can be viewed as a toolbar.

Close
To quit an application and remove its window from the screen. You can also close a file while leaving the application open. The Close button appears in the upper-right corner of the application or worksheet window.

Column selector button
The grey rectangle that appears above each column and displays its column letter.

Comment
An electronic note that can be attached to a cell. Similar to a text box, but can be hidden from view.

Conditional Formulas
A formula which has specific criteria which must be met before the formula will finish calculating.

Contents tab
A Help tab that organizes Excel's help files by topics and subtopics, much like the table of contents in a book or an outline.

Control menu
Contains commands relating to resizing, moving, and closing a window.

Copy
To place a duplicate of a file, or portion thereof, on the Clipboard to be pasted in another location.

Custom View
A customized setting for viewing a worksheet.

Cut
To remove a file, or a portion of a file, and place it on the Clipboard.

D

Data form
A form used by Excel to help enter data into a list.

Data series
The selected data taken from a worksheet and converted into a chart.

Delete
To remove the contents from a cell or an object such as a chart from the worksheet.

Dialog box

A box that offers additional command options for you to review or change before executing the command.

Documentation

The first section of a worksheet. It contains important information such as the spreadsheet's author, purpose, date of creation, file name, macros, and ranges.

Drawing toolbar

Contains tools for creating and formatting shapes, text boxes, and WordArt.

Dummy row/column

A blank row or column at the end of a defined range that holds a place so that Excel can recalculate formulas correctly if a new row or column is added to the range.

E

Edit

To add, delete, or modify cell contents or other elements of a file.

Electronic spreadsheet application

A computer program designed to organize information in columns and rows on a worksheet and facilitate performing rapid and accurate calculations on groups of interrelated numbers.

Ellipsis

Three dots (...) after a command that indicate a dialog box will follow with options for executing the command.

Enter button

Confirms cell entries. The Enter button is located on the formula bar and is symbolized by a check mark.

Exploded pie slice

A pie chart slice that has been dragged away from the rest of the pie to emphasize it.

F

Fields

The type of information which will be organized by the list that is being created.

Fill handle

The small black square at the bottom right corner of the cell pointer. Draging the fill handle copies a cell's contents to adjacent cells or fills a range with series information.

Floating toolbar

A toolbar housed in its own window rather than along an edge of a window. All toolbars in Excel 2000 can be dragged to a floating position.

Folders

Subdivisions of a disk that function as a filing system to help you organize files.

Font

A name given to a collection of text characters of a certain size, weight, and style. Font has become synonymous with typeface. Arial and Times New Roman are examples of font names.

Footer

Contains information towards the bottom or the "foot" of the page.

Format

The way information appears on a page. To format means to change the appearance of data without changing its content.

Formula
A combination of cell addresses and operators that instructs Excel to perform calculations such as adding, subtracting, multiplying, or averaging.

Formula bar
The area below the Formatting toolbar that displays cell contents whether they are labels, values, or formulas. You may enter and edit cell contents in the formula bar rather than in the cell itself.

Function
A built-in formula included in Excel that makes it easy for you to perform common calculations.

G

Go To
A useful command for moving great distances across a worksheet.

Gridlines
Vertical and horizontal lines on a chart that delineate a cell's boundaries.

H

Headers
Information which may be contained at the top, or "head" of the page.

Hyperlink
Text which is linked to another file, and will access that file when clicked, often used on Web pages.

I

Index
A help tab that lists all of Excel's help topics alphabetically.

Input
The data you enter into a worksheet and work with to produce results.

Insertion point
A vertical blinking line on the screen that indicates where text and graphics will be inserted. The insertion point also indicates where an action will begin.

L

Label
Text or numbers that describe the data you place in rows and columns. Labels should be entered in a worksheet first to define the rows and columns and are automatically left-aligned by Excel.

Label prefix
A typed character that marks an entry as a label. For example, if you type an apostrophe before a number, it will be treated as label rather than as a value.

Landscape
A term used to refer to horizontal page orientation; opposite of "portrait," or vertical, orientation.

Launch
To start a program so you can work with it.

Legend
The section of a chart that details which colors or patterns on a chart represent which information.

List
A database which has been created in Excel, to help organize and manage worksheet information.

M

Macro

A set of instructions that automates a specific multistep task that you perform frequently, reducing the process to one command.

Menu

A list of related application commands.

Menu bar

Lists the names of menus containing application commands. Click a menu name on the menu bar to display its list of commands.

Merge and Center command

Combines two or more adjacent cells into a single cell and places the contents of the furthest upper-left cell at the center of the new cell.

Microsoft Clip Gallery

A database of images which may be used to add graphics to your document.

Mouse pointer

The usually arrow-shaped cursor on the screen that you control by guiding the mouse on your desk. You use the mouse pointer to select items, drag objects, choose commands, and start or exit programs. The shape of the mouse pointer can change depending on the task being executed.

N

Name Box

The box at the left end of the formula bar that displays the address of the active cell or the name of a selected range that has been defined and named. You can also use the drop-down arrow in the Name Box to select a named range.

O

Object

An item such as a chart or graphic that that can be relocated and resized independently of the structure of the worksheet.

Office Assistant

An animated representation of the Microsoft Office 2000 help facility. The Office Assistant provides hints, instructions, and a convenient interface between the user and Excel's various help features.

Open

Command used to access a file that has already been created and saved on disk.

Order of operations

The order Excel follows when calculating formulas with multiple operations: 1) exponents, 2) multiplication and division from left to right, 3) addition and subtraction from left to right. In addition, operations inside parenthesis are calculated first, using the above order.

Output

The results produced by calculations done on the input data of a worksheet.

P

Page Break

A set of borders which may be inserted whenever you want to limit the amount of information that appears on the printed page.

Paste

To insert cut or copied data into other cells, worksheets, or workbooks.

Paste Function command
Command that allows you to choose and perform a calculation without entering its formula on the keyboard.

Paste Special command
Allows you to paste the contents of a cell using formatting characteristics that you specify.

Personal Macro Workbook
Allows you to store macros so that they will be available to all Excel workbooks.

PMT Function
A financial function which calculates the periodic payment amount for money borrowed.

Point size
A measurement used for the size of text characters and row height. There are 72 points in one inch.

Portrait
A term used to refer to vertical page orientation; opposite of "landscape," or horizontal, orientation.

Print Preview
Allows you to view your worksheet as it will appear when printed on a sheet of paper.

Print Selection
Allows you to print only the cells which are selected.

Program
A software application that performs specific tasks, such as Microsoft Word or Microsoft Excel.

Programs menu
A menu on the Windows 95 or 98 Start menu that lists the applications on your computer such as Microsoft Excel.

R

Radio button
A small circular button in a dialog box that allows you to turn options on or off.

RAM (random access memory)
The memory that programs use to function while the computer is on. When you shut down the computer, all information in RAM is lost.

Range
A group of two or more cells, usually adjacent.

Range name
A name chosen for a selected group of cells that describes the data they contain.

Record
An individual row of data in a list, with one entry for each field.

Relative cell reference
Allows a formula to be moved to a new location on a worksheet. The formula will then follow the same directional instructions from the new starting point using new cell references.

Reviewing toolbar
Contains commands for inserting, deleting, displaying, and navigating between comments.

Right-click
To click the right mouse button; often used to access specialized menus and shortcuts.

Row height
The measurement of a cell from top to bottom.

Row selector button
The grey rectangle that appears to the left of each row and displays its row number.

Run

To start an application. Also refers to initiating the steps of a macro.

S

Save

Stores changes you have made to a file maintaining the file's current name and location.

Save As

Command used to save a new file for the first time or to create a duplicate copy of a file that has already been saved.

ScreenTip

A brief explanation of a button or object that appears when the mouse pointer is paused over it. Other ScreenTips are accessed by using the What's This? feature on the Help menu or by clicking the question mark button in a dialog box.

Scroll bar

A graphical device for moving vertically and horizontally through a document with the mouse. Scroll bars are located along the right and bottom edges of the document window.

Scroll bar box

A small grey box located inside a scroll bar that indicates your current position relative to the rest of the document window. You can advance a scroll bar box by dragging it, clicking the scroll bar on either side of it, or by clicking the scroll arrows.

Select All button

The grey rectangle in the upper-left corner of the worksheet where the row and column headings meet. Clicking the Select All button highlights the entire worksheet.

Series of labels

A range of incremental labels created by entering the first label in the series and then dragging the fill handle the number of cells desired. Excel automatically enters the remaining labels in order.

Sheet

The term Excel uses to refer to an individual worksheet (sheet 1, sheet 2, etc.).

Sheet tab scrolling buttons

Allow you to access Sheet tabs that are not visible in the window. An Excel workbook opens with only three worksheets, but you may use 255 per workbook.

Sizing handles

Small squares on the corners and sides of a selected object that can be used for changing its dimensions.

Sort command

A command which organizes records in a list by the fields which are specified.

Statistical Functions

Six functions which allow you to calculate various calculations based on the data which appears in a spreadsheet.

Status bar

Displays information regarding your current activity in Excel such as when a cell is ready for editing and when the Number Lock is activated.

Start

To open an application for use.

Start button

A button on the taskbar that accesses a special menu that you use to start programs, find files, access Windows Help and more.

T

Taskbar
A bar, usually located at the bottom of the screen, that contains the Start button, shows which programs are running by displaying their program buttons, and shows the current time.

Text box
A rectangular area in which text is added so that it may be manipulated independently of the rest of a document.

Title bar
The horizontal bar at the top of a window that displays the name of the document or application that appears in the window.

Toolbar
A graphical bar containing buttons that act as shortcuts for common commands.

V

Values
The numbers, formulas, and functions that Excel uses to perform calculations.

Visual Basic
An application which may be used to work with the actual code or programming language of the macro.

W

Web Page
Presents information in a format which may be accessed over the Internet, and may include text, images, etc.

What-If analysis
Technique by which you change certain conditions in a worksheet to see how the changes affect the results of your spreadsheet output.

Window
A rectangular area on the screen in which you view and work on files.

Workbook
An Excel file made up of related worksheets. An individual workbook may contain up to 255 worksheets.

Worksheet
The workspace made up of columns and rows where you enter data to create an electronic spreadsheet.

Worksheet tab
The markers near the bottom of the window that identify which worksheet is currently active. To open a different worksheet, click its tab. Worksheet tabs can be named to reflect their contents.

X

X-axis label
A label summarizing the horizontal (x-axis) data on a chart.

Y

Y-axis label
A label summarizing the vertical (y-axis) data on a chart.

Index

W

Web Page, saving as EX 7.8-7.9

Web Page preview, EX 7.8, 7.16

Web toolbar, EX 1.20

What-If analysis, EX 2.16-2.19

Windows desktop, EX 1.4-1.5

Workbook:
defined, EX 1.2
managing, EX 7.1-7.24
sending via e-mail, EX 7.8

Worksheets:
adding comments to, EX 4.6-4.7
adding new, EX 1.12
closing, EX 1.16-1.19
documenting, EX 1.2
four sections of, EX 1.2
inserting and deleting, EX 7.4-7.5
moving around, EX 1.10-1.13
moving or copying, EX 7.4
opening, EX 1.20-1.21
printing, EX 2.20-2.21
referencing, EX 7.6-7.7
renaming, EX 7.4-7.5
saving, EX 1.16-1.19
saving as a Web page, EX 7.8-7.9
text boxes in, EX 4.2-4.5

World Wide Web, searching in Excel, EX 1.20

Wrapping text, in text boxes, EX 4.2

X

XY chart type, EX 4.16

Z

Zoom setting, EX 7.12-7.13